KS3 MATHS IS EASY

(PROBABILITY & STATISTICS)

www.How2Become.com

As part of this product you have also received **FREE** access to online tests that will help you to pass Key Stage 3 MATHS *(Probability & Statistics).*

To gain access, simply go to:

www.MyEducationalTests.co.uk

Get more products for passing any test at:

www.How2Become.com

Orders: Please contact How2Become Ltd, Suite 14, 50 Churchill Square Business Centre, Kings Hill, Kent ME19 4YU.

You can order through Amazon.co.uk under ISBN: 9781911259282, via the website www.How2Become.com or through Gardners.com.

ISBN: 9781911259282

First published in 2017 by How2Become Ltd.

Copyright © 2017 How2Become.

All rights reserved. Apart from any permitted use under UK copyright law, no part of this publication may be reproduced or transmitted in any form or by any means, electronic or mechanical, including photocopying, recording, or any information, storage or retrieval system, without permission in writing from the publisher or under licence from the Copyright Licensing Agency Limited. Further details of such licenses (for reprographic reproduction) may be obtained from the Copyright Licensing Agency Ltd, Saffron House, 6-10 Kirby Street, London EC1N 8TS.

Typeset for How2Become Ltd by Anton Pshinka.

Printed and bound by CPI Group (UK) Ltd, Croydon, CR0 4YY

Disclaimer

Every effort has been made to ensure that the information contained within this guide is accurate at the time of publication. How2Become Ltd is not responsible for anyone failing any part of any selection process as a result of the information contained within this guide. How2Become Ltd and their authors cannot accept any responsibility for any errors or omissions within this guide, however caused. No responsibility for loss or damage occasioned by any person acting, or refraining from action, as a result of the material in this publication can be accepted by How2Become Ltd.

The information within this guide does not represent the views of any third party service or organisation.

Contains public sector information licensed under the Open Government Licence v3.0.

CONTENTS

Understanding the Curriculum	7
Increase your Chances	17
Learn your Maths Terminology	23
Working out the Probability	27
Mean, Mode, Median and Range	43
Representing Data	
• *Types of Data*	*55*
• *Bars and Pies*	*63*
• *Scatter and Lines*	*85*
• *Frequencies and Tallies*	*103*
• *Pictograms and Other Useful Diagrams*	*123*

UNDERSTANDING THE CURRICULUM

THE NATIONAL CURRICULUM

State-funded schools are governed by a set curriculum of 'core' subjects which form part of a child's education. These core subjects are essential for providing key knowledge and skills, which in turn will help us to produce well-rounded and educated citizens.

In Key Stage 3 (ages 11-14), the core subjects that must be taught in schools include the following:

- **English**
- **Maths**
- **Science**
- **Art and Design**
- **Citizenship**
- **Computing**
- **Design and Technology**
- **Languages**
- **Geography**
- **History**
- **Music**
- **Physical Education**

All schools, from Key Stage 1 to Key Stage 4, must also teach Religious Studies to their students. From the age of 11, children will also be taught Sex Education. However, parents are given the option of pulling their children out from Religious Studies and Sex Education.

THE IMPORTANCE OF MATHS

The subject of maths is an integral part of the national curriculum. Students should be able to understand key concepts and different mathematical formulae, in order to enhance their knowledge and increase their cognitive ability.

UNDERSTANDING THE CURRICULUM

By achieving a strong level of understanding, students are able to convey their mathematical knowledge in a range of other subjects including science, computing and geography.

The fundamental aims of the maths subject include:

- Using arithmetic to solve problems;
- Understanding the difference between accuracy and estimation;
- Expressing arithmetic using algebraic equations and formula;
- Learning how to carefully lay out sets of data using graphs and charts;
- Understanding averages in terms of mean, mode, median and range;
- Improving children's basic mathematical skills, before advancing on to more technical and challenging mathematical concepts;
- Improving children's confidence in their mathematical abilities, allowing them to grasp different topics of maths and how they can apply these techniques to their work.

In Key Stage 3, maths is broken down into several modules:

- **Numbers and Calculations;**
- **Ratio, Proportion and Rates of Change;**
- **Geometry and Measures;**
- **Working with Algebra;**
- **Probability and Statistics.**

The aforementioned modules are all used to teach students the vital skills for both academia and the outside world.

Pupils will be able to recognise different mathematic concepts and apply them to different calculations. In Key Stage 3, it is important that students are able to move fluently through the subject, and demonstrate a wide range of skills.

Key Stage 3 is a crucial time in academic terms, as it prepares students for their GCSEs. Every pupil will be required to take maths as a GCSE, so having a strong knowledge in these starter years at secondary school (KS3) will put students in a strong position for their GCSEs.

MATHS SUBJECT CONTENT

Below we have broken down the aims and objectives of each 'module' for maths. This will give you some idea of what will be assessed, and how study can be improved in different areas of the mathematics subject as a whole.

NUMBERS AND CALCULATIONS

Pupils will be taught how to:
- Apply the concepts of the following mathematical numbers:
    - *Prime numbers, factors, multiples, common factors, common multiples, highest common factor (HCF), lowest common multiple (LCM) and prime factorisation.*
- Use place values for working out decimals, measures and integers of any size.
- Order numbers in terms of positive and negative. Students should also have a strong grasp of mathematical symbols including:
    - $=, \neq, \leq, \geq$
- Use brackets, powers, roots and reciprocals.
- Use different standard units of measure including:
    - *Mass, length, time and money.*
- Round numbers up and down to the correct degree of accuracy. Students will be taught about significant figures and decimal places.
- Correctly use a calculator, and learn all of the key buttons on a scientific calculator.
- Interpret percentages as being 'a number out of 100'. Pupils will also be taught how to use percentages higher than 100%, how to convert a percentage into a fraction or decimal, and how to find the percentage of a number.
- Recognise square and cube numbers, and understanding the importance of powers 2, 3, 4 and 5.
- Interpret and compare numbers in standard form $A \times 10^N$ $1 \leq A < 10$, where N is a positive or negative integer or zero.

UNDERSTANDING THE CURRICULUM

PROBABILITY AND STATISTICS

Pupils will be taught how to:

- Understand the probability of an outcome.
- Record, describe and analyse the frequency of outcomes of simple probability experiments involving randomness, fairness, equally and unequally likely outcomes, using mathematical language, and the use of a probability scale from 0-1.
- Enumerate data and understand information provided in the form of:
  - *Tables, grids, graphs and charts, Venn diagrams and pictograms.*
- Describe, interpret and compare information from graphical representations.
- Understand the mean, mode, median and range of a set of data, and comparing this to other similar data.
- Construct graphs and charts in order to represent a set of data. Pupils should understand what type of graph or chart works best for the data they have collated.

RATIO, PROPORTION AND RATES OF CHANGE

Pupils will be taught how to:

- Change between different standard units. For example:
  - *Length, area, time, volume and mass.*
- Use ratio notation, including reduction to simplest form.
- Use scale factors, scale diagrams and maps.
- Express one quantity as a fraction of another, where the fraction is less than 1 and greater than 1.
- Divide a given quantity into two parts in a given part:part or part:whole ratio; express the division of a quantity into two parts as a ratio.
- Understand that a multiplicative relationship between two quantities can be expressed as a ratio or a fraction.
- Relate the language of ratios and the associated calculations to the arithmetic of fractions and to linear functions.
- Solve problems involving percentage change, including:
  - *Percentage increase, percentage decrease, original value problems and simple interest in financial mathematics.*
- Solve problems involving direct and inverse proportion, including graphical and algebraic representations.
- Use compound units such as speed, unit pricing and density to solve problems.

WORKING WITH ALGEBRA

<u>Pupils will be taught how to:</u>

❑ Use and interpret algebraic notations, including:
- *ab in place of a x b;*
- *3y in place of y + y + y and 3 x y;*
- *a² in place of a x a, a³ in place of a x a x a, a²b in place of a x a x b;*
- $\frac{a}{b}$ *in place of a ÷ b;*
- *Coefficients written as fractions rather than as decimals;*
- *Brackets.*

❑ Substitute numerical values into formulae and expressions, including scientific formulae.

❑ Understand and use the concepts and vocabulary of expressions, equations, inequalities, terms and factors.

❑ Simplify and manipulate algebraic expressions to maintain equivalence by:
- *Collecting like terms;*
- *Multiplying a single term over a bracket;*
- *Taking out common factors;*
- *Expanding products of two or more binomials.*

❑ Recognise, sketch and produce graphs of linear and quadratic functions of one variable with appropriate scaling, using equations in x and y and the Cartesian plane.

❑ Use linear and quadratic graphs to estimate values of y for given values of x and vice versa and to find approximate solutions of simultaneous linear equations.

❑ Recognise arithmetic sequences and find the nth term.

❑ Find approximate solutions to contextual problems from given graphs of a variety of functions, including piece-wise linear, exponential and reciprocal graphs.

❑ Reduce a given linear equation in two variables to the standard form y = mx + c; calculate and interpret gradients and intercepts of graphs of such linear equations numerically, graphically and algebraically.

❑ Recognise geometric sequences and appreciate other sequences that arise.

GEOMETRY AND MEASURES

Pupils will be taught how to:

- Derive and apply formulae to calculate and solve problems involving:
  - *Perimeter and area of triangles, parallelograms, trapezia, volume of cuboids (including cubes) and other prisms (including cylinders).*
- Calculate and solve problems involving: perimeters of 2-D shapes (including circles), areas of circles and composite shapes.
- Draw and measure line segments and angles in geometric figures, including interpreting scale drawings.
- Describe, sketch and draw using conventional terms and notations:
  - *Points, lines, parallel lines, perpendicular lines, right angles, regular polygons, and other polygons that are reflectively and rotationally symmetric.*
- Use the standard conventions for labelling the sides and angles of triangle ABC, and know and use the criteria for congruence of triangles.
- Derive and illustrate properties of triangles, quadrilaterals, circles, and other plane figures [for example, equal lengths and angles] using appropriate language and technologies.
- Use Pythagoras' Theorem and trigonometric ratios in similar triangles to solve problems involving right-angled triangles.
- Use the properties of faces, surfaces, edges and vertices of cubes, cuboids, prisms, cylinders, pyramids, cones and spheres to solve problems in 3-D.
- Interpret mathematical relationships both algebraically and geometrically.
- Identify properties of, and describe the results of, translations, rotations and reflections applied to given figures.
- Identify and construct congruent triangles, and construct similar shapes by enlargement, with and without coordinate grids.
- Apply the properties of angles at a point, angles at a point on a straight line and vertically opposite angles.
- Understand and use the relationship between parallel lines and alternate and corresponding angles.

Maths is not only a core subject in schools, but is also a topic that impacts every aspect of our daily lives. As you can see, it is imperative that students are able to engage in mathematics, in order to improve on vital skills and knowledge.

USING THIS GUIDE

This guide focuses specifically on Key Stage 3 Maths (Probability and Statistics). This book will cover everything you will need to know in terms of probabilities, averages, graphs and charts.

REMEMBER – It's really important that you have a good mathematical understanding, as this will help you through other school subjects, as well as in day-to-day activities.

HOW WILL I BE ASSESSED?

In Key Stage 3, children will be assessed based on Levels. These years do not count towards anything, and are simply a reflection of progression and development. That is to say, the first years of secondary school are in place in order to determine whether pupils are meeting the minimum requirements, and are therefore an integral stage for preparing pupils for their GCSE courses.

Although these years do not count towards any final results, they do go a long way in deciphering which GCSEs you will pick up. For example, if you were excelling in maths at KS3, you could consider taking this subject at A-Level, or even continue with it during your higher education!

The subjects that you choose at GCSE will have an impact on your future aspirations, including further education and career opportunities.

You will be monitored and assessed throughout these schooling years, via the following:

- Ongoing teacher assessments;
- Term progress reports;
- Summative assessments at the end of each academic year.

UNDERSTANDING THE CURRICULUM

By the end of Key Stage 3, pupils are expected to achieve Levels 5 or 6.

THE REVISION SERIES

INCREASE YOUR CHANCES

Below is a list of GOLDEN NUGGETS that will help YOU and your CHILD to prepare for the Key Stage 3 maths.

Golden Nugget 1 – Revision timetables

When it comes to revising, preparation is key. That is why you need to sit down with your child and come up with an efficient and well-structured revision timetable.

It is important that you work with your child to assess their academic strengths and weaknesses, in order to carry out these revision sessions successfully.

TIP – Focus on their weaker areas first!

TIP – Create a weekly revision timetable to work through different subject areas.

TIP – Spend time revising with your child. Your child will benefit from your help and this is a great way for you to monitor their progress.

Golden Nugget 2 – Understanding the best way your child learns

There are many different ways to revise when it comes to exams, and it all comes down to picking a way that your child will find most useful.

Below is a list of the common learning styles that you may want to try with your child:

- **Visual** – the use of pictures and images to remember information.
- **Aural** – the use of sound and music to remember information.
- **Verbal** – the use of words, in both speech and writing, to understand information.
- **Social** – working together in groups.
- **Solitary** – working and studying alone.

INCREASE YOUR CHANCES

Popular revision techniques include: *mind mapping, flash cards, making notes, drawing flowcharts,* and *diagrams.* You could instruct your child on how to turn diagrams and pictures into words, and words into diagrams. Try as many different methods as possible, to see which style your child learns from the most.

> **TIP** – *Work out what kind of learner your child is. What method will they benefit from the most?*
>
> **TIP** – *Try a couple of different learning aids and see if you notice a change in your child's ability to understand what is being taught.*

Golden Nugget 3 – Break times

Allow your child plenty of breaks when revising. It's important not to overwork your child.

> **TIP** – *Practising for 10 to 15 minutes per day will improve your child's reading ability.*
>
> **TIP** – *Keep in mind that a child's retention rate is usually between 30 to 50 minutes. Any longer than this, and your child will start to lose interest.*

Golden Nugget 4 – Practice, practice and more practice!

Purchase past practice papers. Practice papers are still a fantastic way for you to gain an idea of how your child is likely to be tested.

Golden Nugget 5 – Understanding different areas in maths

As with any subject, maths has a range of different modules. Therefore, your child may find one module easier than another. We recommend that you spend time focusing on one module at a time. This will ensure that your child knows everything they should about each module – before moving on to the next.

> **TIP** – *Know what modules you need to focus on!*

Golden Nugget 6 – Improve their confidence

Encourage your child to interact with you, their peers and their teachers. If they are struggling, they need to be able to reach out and ask for help. By asking for help, they will be able to work on their weaknesses, and therefore increase their overall performance and confidence.

> **TIP** – Talk to your child and work through different maths questions with them.

Golden Nugget 7 – Stay positive!

The most important piece of preparation advice we can give you, is to make sure that your child is positive and relaxed about these tests.

Don't let assessments worry you, and certainly don't let them worry your child.

> **TIP** – Make sure the home environment is as comfortable and relaxed as possible for your child.

Golden Nugget 8 – Answer the easier questions first

A good tip to teach your child is to answer all the questions they find easiest first. That way, they can swiftly work through the paper, before attempting the questions they struggle with.

> **TIP** – Get your child to undergo a practice paper. Tell them to fill in the answers that they find the easiest first. That way, you can spend time helping your child with the questions they find more difficult.
>
> Spend some time working through the questions they find difficult and make sure that they know how to work out the answer.

INCREASE YOUR CHANCES

Golden Nugget 9 – Understanding mathematical terminology

The next section is a glossary containing all the mathematical terminology that your child should familiarise themselves with.

Sit down with your child and learn as many of these KEY TERMS as you can.

TIP – *Why not make your child's learning fun? Write down all of the terms and cut them out individually. Do the same for the definitions.*

Get your child to try and match the KEY TERM with its definition. Keep playing this game until they get them all right!

Golden Nugget 10 – Check out our other revision resources

We have a range of other KS3 Maths resources to help your child prepare for EVERY stage of their mathematical learning.

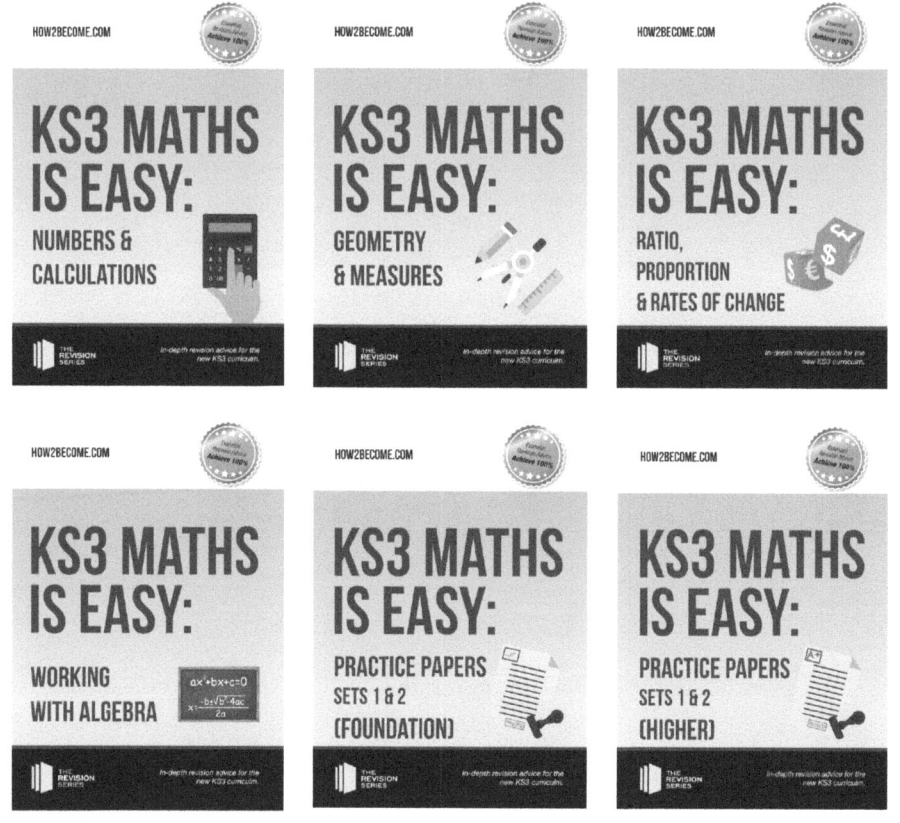

THE
REVISION
SERIES

LEARN YOUR MATHS TERMINOLOGY

ACUTE ANGLES	An angle less than 90°.
ALGEBRA	The part of maths where symbols and letters are used to represent numbers.
AREA	A measurement of a surface. The area of a square, you would multiply the height by the width.
BIDMAS	Brackets, Indices, Division, Multiplication, Addition, Subtraction. This shows the order you would complete a calculation with many operations.
CIRCUMFERENCE	The distance around something. It is the enclosing boundary of a curved geometric figure.
COMPOUND SHAPE	A compound shape includes two or more simple shapes.
CUBED NUMBERS	A cube is a number multiplied by itself, three times.
DECIMAL PLACES	The position of a digit to the right of a decimal point.
DECIMAL	A type of number, for example 0.5 is equivalent to 50%.
DIAMETER	A straight line passing side-to-side through the middle of a circle.
EQUILATERAL TRIANGLE	A type of triangle. All sides and angles are of equal value. All angles are 60°.
ESTIMATING	A rough calculation or guess.
FACTOR	A factor is a number that can be divided wholly into another number. For example, 4 is a factor of 8.
FRACTIONS	A type of number, for example ½ is equivalent to a half.
FREQUENCY	The frequency of a specific data is the number of times that number occurs. (Frequent).
HIGHEST COMMON FACTOR (HCF)	To find the HCF, you need to find all of the factors of two or more numbers, and then see which number is the highest.

LEARN YOUR MATHS TERMINOLOGY

IMPERIAL UNITS	Imperial units of length, mass and capacity. Includes inch, foot, yard, ounce, pound, stone, pint and gallon.
ISOSCELES TRIANGLE	A type of triangle. Two sides and angles are of the same value.
LOWEST COMMON MULTIPLE (LCM)	To find the LCM, you need to find all of the multiples of two or more numbers, and then work out the lowest number in common.
MEAN	A type of average. Add up all of the numbers and divide it by how many numbers there are.
MEDIAN	A type of average. Rearrange the numbers in ascending order. What number is in the middle?
METRIC UNITS	Metric units of length, mass and capacity. Includes mm, cm, km, mg, g, kg, ml and litres.
MODE	A type of average. What number occurs the most?
MULTIPLE	A multiple simply means 'times tables'. The multiples of 2 are 2, 4, 6, 8 and so on.
NEGATIVE NUMBER	A negative number is a number less than 0. On a scale, positive numbers move to the right, and negative numbers move to the left. Indicated by the sign '-'. For example, -4.
OBTUSE ANGLE	A type of angle. An obtuse angle is more than 90° but less than 180°.
PARALLEL LINES	Parallel lines are two or more lines that are always the same distance apart, and never touch.
PERIMETER	A measurement of a surface. The line forming the boundary of a closed geometrical figure.
PERPENDICULAR LINES	A perpendicular line is two more lines that meet at a right angle (90°).
PI	The mathematic constant 3.14159... The ratio of a circle's circumference to its diameter.

POSITIVE NUMBER	A positive number is a number more than 0. On a scale, positive numbers move to the right, and negative numbers move to the left.
PROBABILITY	The extent to whether something is likely to occur.
RADIUS	The radius is a straight line from the mid-point of a circle, to the outer edge of the circle.
RANGE	A type of average. The range between the largest number and the smallest number.
RATIO	The quantitative relation between two amounts showing the number of times one value contains or is contained within the other.
REFLEX ANGLE	A type of angle. A reflex angle is more than 180° but less than 360°.
RIGHT-ANGLED TRIANGLE	A type of triangle. A triangle that has a 90° angle.
SCALENE TRIANGLE	A triangle with no equal angles or equal length sides.
SIGNIFICANT FIGURES	The digits carrying meaning. This allows us to get a rough idea. For example, 48,739. The '4' is a significant figure because it represents 40 thousand.
SIMPLIFYING FRACTIONS	A way of making a fraction easier to read by finding a whole number that can be divided equally into both the denominator and numerator. For example, 12/24 can be simplified to 1/2. Both '12' and '24' can be divided by 12.
SQUARED NUMBER	A square number is the number that is reached when multiplying two of the same numbers together. For example 9 is the square number of 3 x 3.
SYMMETRY	Symmetry is when one shape becomes exactly like another if it's flipped or rotated.
VOLUME	The amount of space that a shape or object occupies. Contained within a container.

THE REVISION SERIES

WORKING OUT THE PROBABILITY

WHAT IS PROBABILITY?

Probability is all about estimating how likely (probable) an event is likely to happen. It is the 'Maths of Chance'.

Probability is a great concept to predict something happening.

Below we have outlined some 'events' where you'll need to use probability to estimate how likely something is to happen:

- The odds of a coin landing on heads (or tails);
- The odds of a die landing on a particular number;
- The odds of it raining in the first week of December.

All probabilities are between 0 and 1.

Probabilities can be written in four different ways:

1) Fractions;
2) Percentages;
3) Decimals;
4) Probability scale.

WORKING OUT THE PROBABILITY

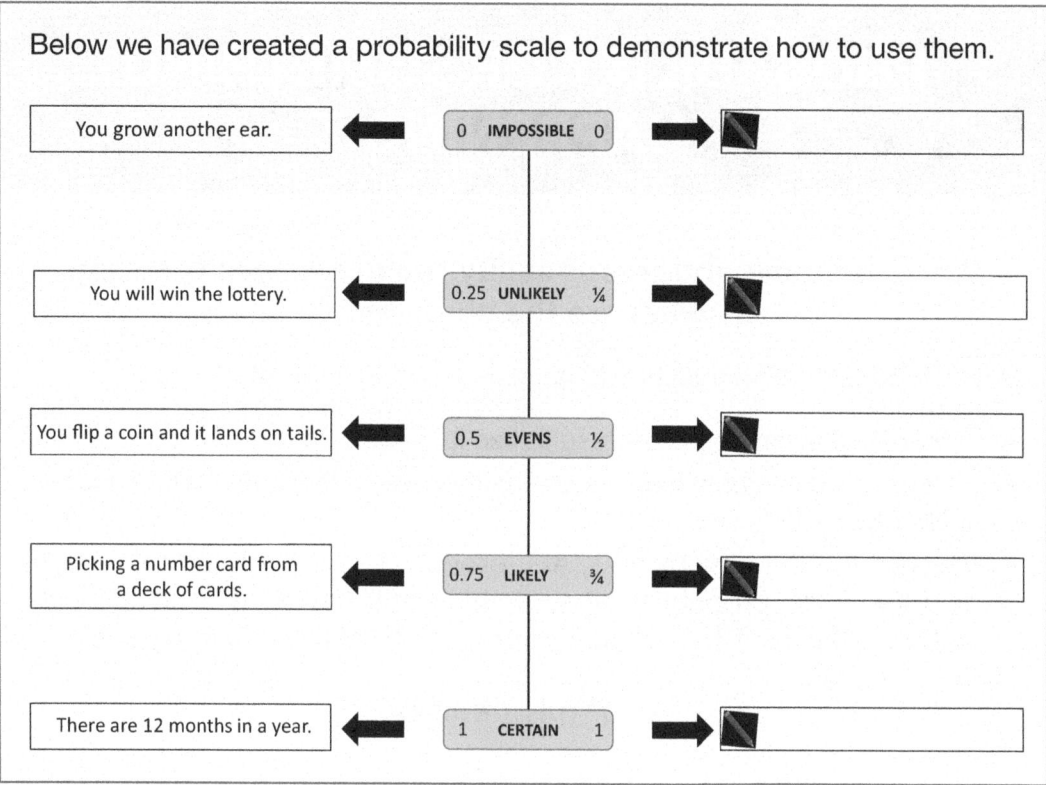

When dealing with probabilities, sometimes you want a quick way to write something down. This is called **'shorthand'**.

You can use shorthand to talk about something instead of writing out lots of words.

For example:

Instead of saying 'the probability of a die landing on an even number is 0.5, you can write it out as follows:

$$P(E) = 0.5$$

P = Probability

E = Even number on a die

PROBABILITY OF SOMETHING HAPPENING

When we think about probability, we are basically saying 'what are the chances?'

When looking at probabilities, we can look at it in several ways:

- If there is only one possible result, then it will add up to 1.
- If there is a 0.24 chance of something happening, there is a 0.76 chance of it NOT happening (1 − 0.24 = 0.76).
- As you should know by now, ALL probabilities will add up to 1. So, if you know the probability of something that happens, then you can subtract this by 1 to find out the probability of it NOT happening.

1 − P (probability)

EQUAL CHANCE	UNEQUAL CHANCE
The probability of something which has the same level of chance, is known as **'EQUAL PROBABILITY'**.	The probability of something which has different levels of chance, is known as **'UNEQUAL PROBABILITY'**.

I can demonstrate this with two examples.

1. Throwing a die
You have an equal chance of landing on an even number as you do an odd number.

2. Tossing a coin
You have an equal chance of the coin landing on heads as it does tails.

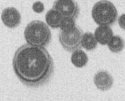

For example:

If you have a bag of 10 buttons (3 are red, 2 are blue, 1 is orange, and the rest are yellow) you have different chances of picking out different coloured buttons.

FORMULA
To work out the probability:

$$\frac{\textit{Number of ways something can happen}}{\textit{Total number of possible outcomes}}$$

WORKING OUT THE PROBABILITY

RELATIVE FREQUENCY

Theoretical probability is what you EXPECT to happen. Experimental probability is what ACTUALLY happens.

Relative frequency is determining the likely outcome of something.

Ethan throws a die. He is trying to work out the probability of the die landing on the number 4. Ethan says:

"The probability that the die lands on a 4 is 1 out of 6 (1/6). That means if I throw the die 6 times, I should get exactly one 4."

Theoretically, Ethan is correct. However, if Ethan runs this experiment, this might not be the case. You won't always get exactly one 4.

If Ethan rolls the die 24 times, how many times can Ethan expect the die to land on the number 2?

- If there is a 1 in 6 chance of the die landing on the number 2, this means that for every roll, Ethan has the same chance.

- In 24 rolls, Ethan can expect to roll the number 2 four times.

- Every time Ethan repeats this experiment, his results will of course change!

WORKING OUT THE OUTCOME

When it comes to probability, most of the time there will be multiple outcomes.

If you are working with two things, then you will have to work out the multiple outcomes that can occur.

Let's use two coins and see what the possible outcomes are:

HEADS	HEADS
HEADS	TAILS
TAILS	HEADS
TAILS	TAILS

WORKING OUT THE PROBABILITY

WHAT DO WE KNOW FROM THE LAST PAGE?

- There are four possible outcomes:
    - HH   HT   TH   TT
- The probability of two coins both landing on heads is ¼.
- The probability of two coins both landing on tails is ¼.
- The probability of two coins landing on heads then tails is ¼.
- The probability of two coins landing on tails then heads is ¼.

Let's try a trickier list of outcomes.

Below are two spinners. One spinner contains the numbers 1-4, and the other spinner contains the letters A-D.

 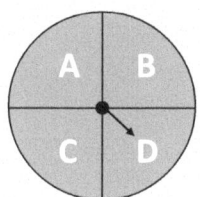

Using a table, we can visualise the probability of two spinners landing on different outcomes.

	A	B	C	D
1	1A	1B	1C	1D
2	2A	2B	2C	2D
3	3A	3B	3C	3D
4	4A	4B	4C	4D

There are 16 possible outcomes (4 x 4). Any number could appear with any letter.

The probability of spinning the number 4 and the letter C is 1 out of 16 (1/16).

$$P(4C) = 1/16$$

QUESTION 1

For the following statement, tick which answer is correct.

The total of the probability of all possible outcomes equals:

a) 0.5 ☐

b) 2 ☐

c) 1.5 ☐

d) 1 ☐

QUESTION 2

For the following statement, tick which answer is correct.

*The probability that Mark will finish his Maths homework on time is 16%. What is the probability that Mark **won't** finish his homework on time?*

a) 1 ☐

b) 0.16 ☐

c) 94% ☐

d) 84% ☐

WORKING OUT THE PROBABILITY

QUESTION 3

Below are cards each with a letter of the word 'PROBABILITY'.

Read each question and write your answer in the box provided.

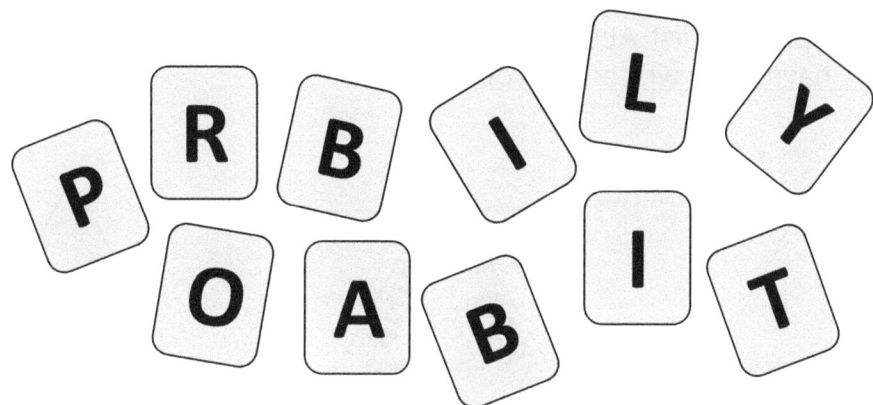

a) What is the probability that the letter 'Y' is chosen?

b) What is the probability of choosing the letter 'B'?

c) Finish the probability:

P(vowel) =

d) Finish the probability:

P(A-I) =

QUESTION 4

Below are three spinners. Spinner 1 contains the numbers 1-3. Spinner 2 contains the names of three different colours. Spinner 3 contains the letters A-C.

Using the spinners, list ALL of the possibilities. <u>The possible outcomes for number 1 have been written for you.</u>

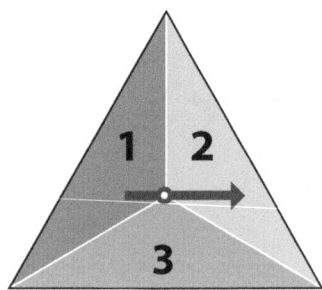 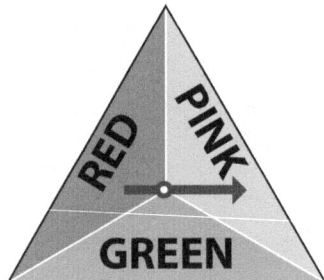 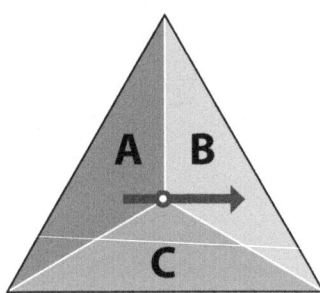

1RA
1RB
1RC
1PA
1PB
1PC
1GA
1GB
1GC

WORKING OUT THE PROBABILITY

QUESTION 5

For the following sentences, circle whether you think the statement is certain, likely, evens, unlikely or impossible.

a) Picking a king in a deck of cards.

    CERTAIN   LIKELY   EVENS   UNLIKELY   IMPOSSIBLE

b) It will rain in December.

    CERTAIN   LIKELY   EVENS   UNLIKELY   IMPOSSIBLE

c) Pigs will fly.

    CERTAIN   LIKELY   EVENS   UNLIKELY   IMPOSSIBLE

QUESTION 6

Samuel plays a game of noughts and crosses with his friend, Pete. In the last 6 weeks, Samuel has won 6 games. His chance of winning the next game is 0.25.

a) What is Samuel's chance of NOT winning?

b) How many games have they played so far?

c) If Pete had won 50% of the games they have played, how many games have they drawn?

QUESTION 7

Rachel has a bag of buttons. Each button has a number.

6	5	9	4	1	3	6
5	7	9	8	2	5	5
6	9	1	2	9	4	6
3	7	9	5	4	1	2

Rachel picks a button out of a bag at random. What is the probability of picking the following? Simplify your answers.

a) P(odd number) =

b) P(even number) =

c) P(number ≤ 5) =

d) P(number ≥ 5) =

QUESTION 8

There are 6 black balls and 4 white balls.

Using the space below to show your working, answer the questions below.

a) What is the probability of picking a white ball? Write your answer as a decimal.

b) If the number of white balls increased by 6, and the number of black balls increased by two, which ball is more likely to be picked at random? Explain your answer.

c) Using your answer to part b, a black ball is picked at random and left out of the bag. Two white balls are picked at random and left out of the bag. A black and white ball are picked at random and left out the bag. What is the probability of choosing a black ball?

Answers

Q1.

D = 1

Q2.

D = 84%

Q3.

a) 1 out of 11 OR 1/11

b) 2 out of 11 OR 2/11

c) P(vowel) = 4/11

d) P(A-I) = 5/11

Q4.

1RA	2RA	3RA
1RB	2RB	3RB
1RC	2RC	3RC
1PA	2PA	3PA
1PB	2PB	3PB
1PC	2PC	3PC
1GA	2GA	3GA
1GB	2GB	3GB
1GC	2GC	3GC

WORKING OUT THE PROBABILITY

Q5.

a) Unlikely

b) Likely

c) Impossible

Q6.

a) 0.75

b) 24

   (6 ÷ 0.25)

c) 6

   (24 games in total. Pete won half (12). Samuel has won 0.25 (24 ÷ 100 x 25 = 6). So 24 – 12 – 6 = 6. So they drew 6 games.)

Q7.

a) P(odd number) = 17/28

b) P(even number) = 11/28 or 6/14 or 3/7

c) P(number ≤ 5) = 16/28 or 8/14 or 4/7

d) P(number ≥ 5) = 17/28

Q8.

a) 0.4 or 2/5

b) Picking a white ball is more likely to happen. If you increased 4 white balls by 6, you would have 10 white balls. If you increased the 6 black balls by 2, you would have 8 black balls. So the odds of picking a white ball is 10/18.

c) 6/13

HOW ARE YOU GETTING ON?

MEAN, MODE, MEDIAN AND RANGE

FINDING THE AVERAGE

Working out the average helps you understand data more clearly. There are different types of averages.

- Mean
- Mode
- Median
- Range

Check out our Youtube channel **CAREERVIDZ** for more information on averages.

HOW TO REMEMBER THE DIFFERENT TYPES OF AVERAGE

Mean = add then divide!

Mode = **Mo**st!

Median = **Mid**dle!

Range = high and low!

MEAN, MODE, MEDIAN AND RANGE

WHAT IS THE MEAN?

The **MEAN** is the most common form of average.
To calculate the mean all you need to do is **ADD UP** all of the numbers, and then **DIVIDE** the sum by how many numbers there are.

MEAN = sum of numbers ÷ amount of numbers

EXAMPLE

| 6 | 9 | 12 | 21 | 34 | 27 | 23 | 20 |

To work out the mean:

STEP 1 – Add up all of the numbers.
6 + 9 + 12 + 21 + 34 + 27 + 23 + 20 = 152

STEP 2 – Divide the sum by how many numbers there are.
152 ÷ 8 = 19

ACTIVITY TIME!

Can you work out what the mean is from this set of data?

ANSWER

| 11 | 13 | 8 | 18 | 21 | 35 | 34 |

WHAT IS THE MODE?

The MODE is the value that occurs the most number of times.

This is the ONLY average that can have multiple values.

MODE = **MO**ST

EXAMPLE

| 5 | 7 | 13 | 11 | 13 | 7 | 1 | 13 |

To work out the mode:

STEP 1 – rearrange the numbers in ascending order.
1   5   7   7   11   13   13   13

STEP 2 – What number occurs the most?
The number 13 occurs three times. No other number occurs more. 13 is the mode.

ACTIVITY TIME!

Can you work out what the mode is from this set of data?

| 24 | 17 | 9 | 24 | 32 | 31 | 22 | ANSWER

MEAN, MODE, MEDIAN AND RANGE

WHAT IS THE MEDIAN?

The **MEDIAN** is the number in the middle, after you've arranged the numbers in ascending order.

MEDIAN = **MID**DLE

EXAMPLE

| 5 | 7 | 13 | 11 | 13 | 7 | 1 | 13 |

To work out the median:

STEP 1 – rearrange the numbers in ascending order.
1 5 7 7 11 13 13 13

STEP 2 – What number is in the middle?
The numbers 7 and 11 are in the middle. To work out the middle number, add up the numbers and then divide it by how many numbers there are: 7 + 11 = 18
18 ÷ 2 = 9. So, **9** is the middle number.

ACTIVITY TIME!

Can you work out what the mode is from this set of data?

ANSWER

| 24 | 17 | 9 | 24 | 32 | 31 | 22 |

WHAT IS THE RANGE?

The RANGE is the difference between the highest value and the lowest value.

To work out the range, subtract the lowest value from the highest value.

Highest value – lowest value

EXAMPLE

| 5 | 7 | 13 | 11 | 13 | 7 | 1 | 13 |

To work out the range:

STEP 1 – subtract the lowest number from the highest number.
13 – 1 = 12

So the range for this set of data is **12**.

ACTIVITY TIME!

Can you work out what the range is from this set of data?

ANSWER

| 32 | 53 | 78 | 13 | 75 | 35 | 54 |

MEAN, MODE, MEDIAN AND RANGE

Question Time!

QUESTION 1

For the following questions, you need to fill in the missing number on the blank cards.

a) If the mean of this set of data is 19, what is the missing number?

b) If the mean and range of this set of data is equal, what is the missing number?

c) If the mean of this set of data is 13, and the range is 19, what are the two missing numbers, assuming that both these numbers are the same value?

| 10 | 12 | 18 | 26 | 14 | 10 | MISSING NUMBER | MISSING NUMBER |

QUESTION 2

Below are the amounts spent in the last week.

£15.50	£0.50
£4.00	£11.50
£2.50	£30.50
£11.50	£40.00
£25.00	£20.50

a) What is the mean amount spent in the last week?

b) What is the mode amount spent in the last week?

c) What is the range amount across the week?

d) What is the median amount spent in the last week?

MEAN, MODE, MEDIAN AND RANGE

QUESTION 3

Below are three empty boxes. Write three **consecutive numbers** so that the **mean** of the three numbers is **28**.

QUESTION 4

The data below shows the temperature changes per hour.

TIME	TEMPERATURES
07:00	1°C
08:00	2°C
09:00	7°C
10:00	10°C
11:00	11°C
12:00	13°C
13:00	12°C

Jacob and Henry are arguing about the average temperature.
Henry says:
 "The mean temperature is greater than the median".
Jacob disagrees.
Using mathematical calculations, explain whether Henry is right or wrong.

_____
_____
_____
_____

QUESTION 5

Below shows the scores in a Science and History test. Use this information to answer the following questions. Test scores are out of 150.

SCIENCE	68	86	142	35	125	116	75	108	86	74
HISTORY	54	85	49	109	67	85	46	95	126	148

a) Complete the table.

	MEAN SCORE	MODE SCORE	MEDIAN SCORE	RANGE SCORE
SCIENCE				
HISTORY				

b) You are asked to analyse the test scores in the first table. Out of the following, **tick** which type of average do you think is best to compare the test results? **Write** your reasons why.

Mean ☐

Mode ☐

Median ☐

Range ☐

_____

_____

_____

_____

MEAN, MODE, MEDIAN AND RANGE

Answers

Q1.

a) 40

b) 4

c) 7 and 7

Q2.

a) £16.15

b) £11.50

c) £39.50

d) £13.50

Q3.

27, 28, 29

Q4.

Henry is wrong.

The mean of this set of data is:
- 1 + 2 + 7 + 10 + 11 + 13 + 12 = 56
- 56 ÷ 7 = 8
- So, the mean is 8

The median of this set of data is:
- 1   2   7   10   11   12   13
- The **mid**dle number is 10. So, this is the median.

Therefore, Henry is wrong. The mean is not higher than the median.

Q5.

a) Your table should look like this:

	MEAN SCORE	MODE SCORE	MEDIAN SCORE	RANGE SCORE
SCIENCE	91.5	86	86	107
HISTORY	86.4	85	85	102

b) *This is based on your personal opinion. You could have ticked any answer so long as you supported your answer with logical reasoning.*

For example:

- The mean is an average that allows you to take into account all of the 'actual' test scores.

- The median and the range would allow you to analyse the results as a whole, and highlight the difference in marks in order to make the most out of the information.

- The mode allows you to see which score appears the most frequent. Although, this wouldn't give you an overall impression of everyone's results, it does allow you to analyse frequency.

HOW ARE YOU GETTING ON?

TYPES OF DATA

(Representing Data)

TYPES OF DATA

Data is all about COLLECTING INFORMATION.

When you have collected data, you have to know what to do with it. This process of collecting and recording data is the easy part. What you then have to do is **INTERPRET** the data.

Data can either be **PRIMARY** or **SECONDARY**.

PRIMARY DATA	SECONDARY DATA
Primary data is data that YOU have collected.	Secondary data is data that has been collected by SOMEONE ELSE.
Sources of primary data: • Questionnaires • Surveys • Experiments • Observations • Interviews • Focus groups	Sources of secondary data: • Books • Articles • Newspapers • Websites • Journals

TYPES OF DATA

Data can either be **QUALITATIVE** or **QUANTITATIVE**.

QUALITATIVE DATA	QUANTITATIVE DATA
Qualitative data is all about words and detail to describe something.	Quantitative data is all about numbers and statistics.
Qualitative = Quality of description	*Quantitative = quantities and numbers*
Unlike quantitative data, it doesn't use numbers.	Anything that can be measured using numbers, will use quantitative methods.
For example:	For example:
• Appearance • Texture • Taste • Smell • Scenery • Gender	• Length • Height • Weight • Area • Volume • Cost

Quantitative data can be either **DISCRETE** or **CONTINUOUS**.

DISCRETE DATA	CONTINUOUS DATA
Discrete data works with whole numbers. It is data that can be recorded **EXACTLY**.	Continuous data is data which can take any value (within any range).
For example:	For example:
• The number of students in a classroom • The results of throwing a die • Number of goals scored in a football game • Number of points in a game of Scrabble	• A person's height • An age of a person • Time taken to finish a race • The weight of something

Question Time!

QUESTION 1

For the following sentences, work out whether it is **PRIMARY** data or **SECONDARY** data.

	PRIMARY	SECONDARY
a) An experiment conducted by a scientist	☐	☐
b) A magazine article about new school curriculums.	☐	☐
c) An experiment conducted by you.	☐	☐
d) Conducting a new interview about school uniforms.	☐	☐

QUESTION 2

Which of the following is **continuous** data?

The horse had won 4 races. ☐

The horse weighs 120.4 kilograms. ☐

The horse gave birth to 1 foal. ☐

The horse has 4 hooves. ☐

QUESTION 3

What is the difference between **discrete** and **continuous** data? Give an example of each.

_____
_____
_____
_____
_____

QUESTION 4

What is the difference between **qualitative** and **quantitative** data? Give an example of each.

_____
_____
_____
_____
_____

QUESTION 5

Give two advantages and two disadvantages of using **primary** and **secondary** data.

_____
_____
_____
_____
_____
_____

Answers

Q1.

	PRIMARY	SECONDARY
a) An experiment conducted by a scientist		✓
b) A magazine article about new school curriculums.		✓
c) An experiment conducted by you.	✓	
d) Conducting a new interview about school uniforms.	✓	

Q2.

Which of the following is **continuous** data?

The horse had won 4 races.	
The horse weighs 120.4 kilograms.	✓
The horse gave birth to 1 foal.	
The horse has four hooves.	

Q3.

Discrete data can only take particular values using whole numbers (for example, 5 and 6). Whereas continuous data is able to take values in the range of whole numbers (for example 5.5).

TYPES OF DATA 61

Q4.

Qualitative data is all about the quality of data. It often uses words to describe something. For example, describing a person's appearance. Whereas quantitative data is all about quantities – it uses numbers and statistics to demonstrate particular data. For example, counting the number of times a car passes by.

Q5.

- Advantage 1 for using primary data = it relates directly to the person's own study.
- Advantage 2 for using primary data = you have collected your own unique research about a topic.

- Advantage 1 for using secondary data = easily accessible.
- Advantage 2 for using secondary data = saves times.

- Disadvantage 1 for using primary data = can be time consuming.
- Disadvantage 2 for using primary data = it will be hard to collect enough data to form a valid conclusion.

- Disadvantage 1 for using secondary data = you are basing your own understanding on someone else's work.
- Disadvantage 2 for using secondary data = it can be difficult to make sure the source is credible.

HOW ARE YOU GETTING ON?

THE REVISION SERIES

BARS AND PIES
(Representing Data)

BAR CHARTS

One of the easiest ways to display data is through the use of a **BAR CHART**.

Bars are used on a graph to show the frequency of something (i.e. how many).

EXAMPLE

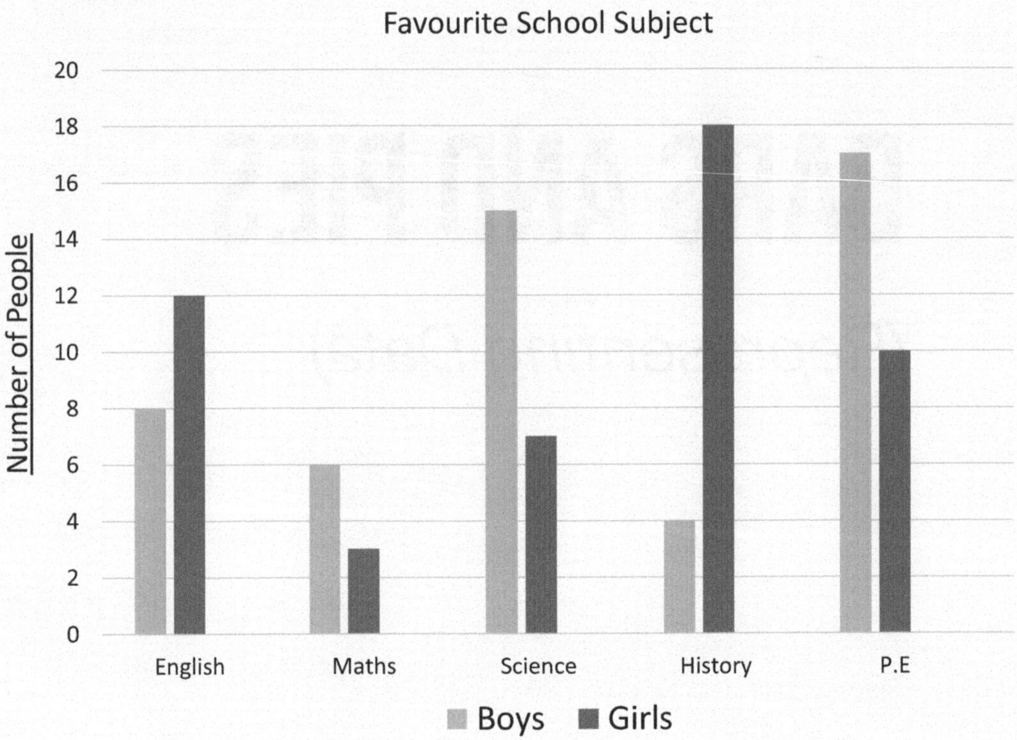

Favourite School Subject

Subject	Boys	Girls
English	8	12
Maths	6	3
Science	15	7
History	4	18
P.E	17	10

In this bar chart, we are looking at the data for people's favourite school subject!

BARS AND PIES

BREAKDOWN OF BAR CHART

- A title is placed at the top of the chart to identify what the chart is representing.
- A label on the left-hand side of the table shows that the numbers are representing the number of people.
- The label at the bottom of the table represents the data for both boys and girls.
- There are 5 categories along the bottom of the chart – English, Maths, Science, History and P.E.
- There are two bars for each subject – the first bar is the result for boys, and the second is the results of the girls. This allows you to compare data not only by subject, but by gender.

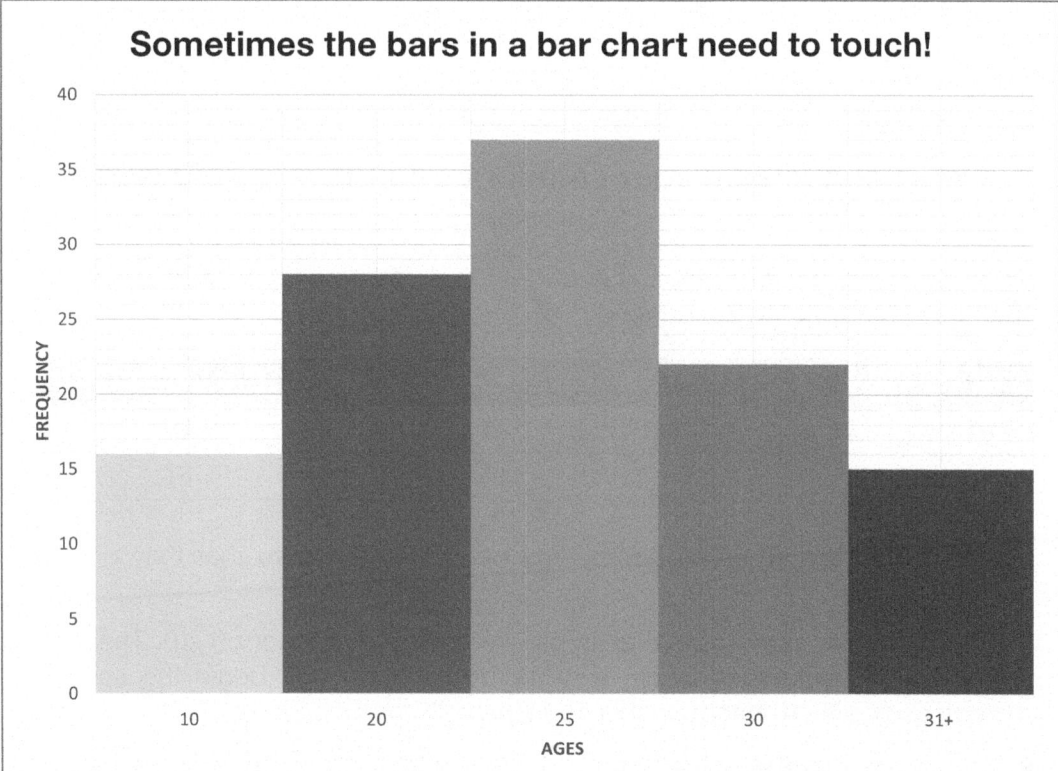

As you can see, the bars NEED to touch because the numbers are covering a RANGE of different ages.

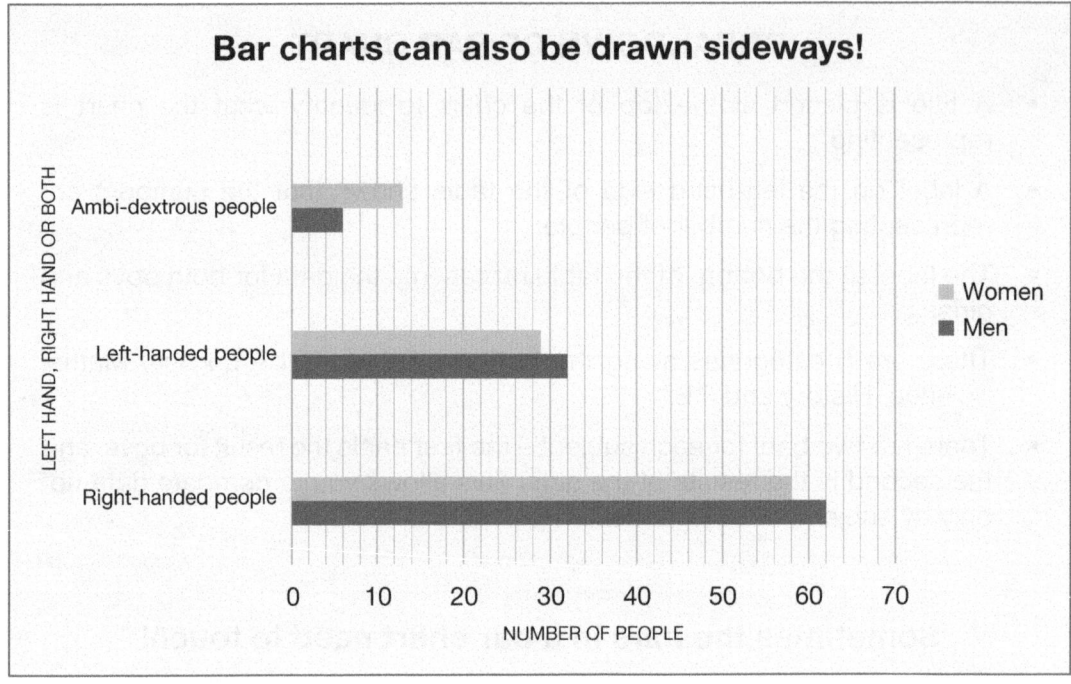

You need to split your categories so that they DO NOT overlap!

When you record your data, it is important that you categorise your results so that they fit only in **ONE** category!

Test scores	0 – 10	11 – 20	21 – 30	31 – 40	41 – 50
Boys	23	19	12	11	35
Girls	15	8	14	6	57

- As you create your categories, you need to make sure that they do not overlap.
- For example, in the above example we have the category 0 -10. The next category would then begin with 11. You would NOT begin the second category with 10 because this conflicts with the first category!
- The issue with this, of course, is that you lose some of your accuracy.

BARS AND PIES

PIE CHARTS

Another way to display data is via **PIE CHARTS**.

This chart is named so because it looks very much like a pie!

EXAMPLE

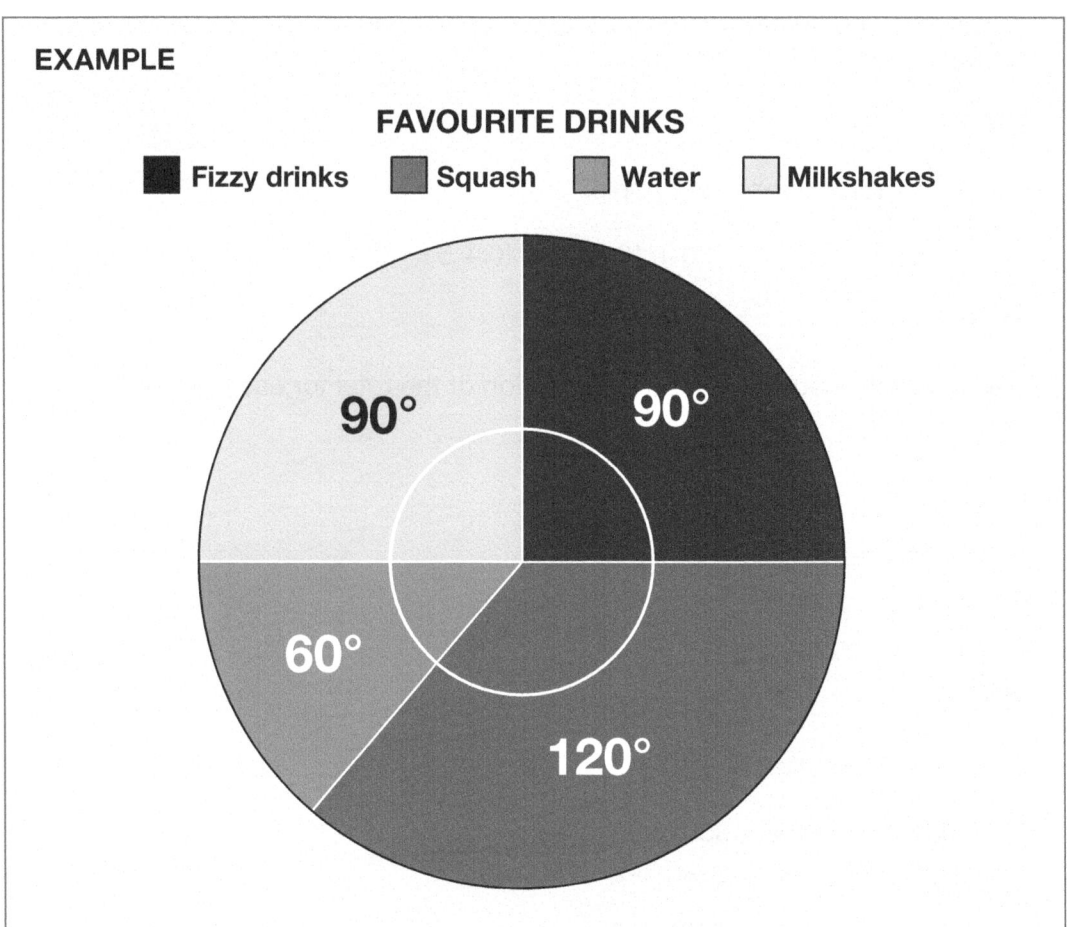

TOTAL of everything is ALWAYS 360°.

How do I construct a pie chart?

In order to work out the size of each sector of the pie chart, you need to work out what angle needs to represent each sector.

GRADE	A	B	C	D	F
FREQUENCY	25	10	50	10	5

To put the above information into a pie chart, you should follow the steps below:

STEP 1

Add up the total number of people.

$$25 + 10 + 50 + 10 + 5 = 100$$

STEP 2

Next, you will need to work out the fraction of the total for each grade.

- Grade A = 25/100
- Grade B = 10/100
- Grade C = 50/100
- Grade D = 10/100
- Grade F = 5/100

STEP 3

Multiply each fraction by 360°.

- Grade A = 25/100 x 360° = 90°
- Grade B = 10/100 x 360° = 36°
- Grade C = 50/100 x 360° = 180°
- Grade D = 10/100 x 360° = 36°
- Grade F = 5/100 x 360° = 18°

So, you now have the angles of each segment.

BARS AND PIES 69

Using the information from the previous page, you will be able to form your pie chart.

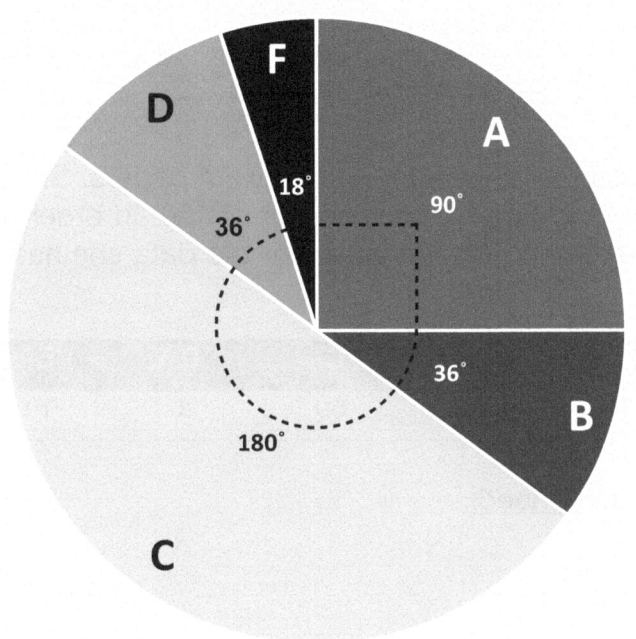

Question Time!

QUESTION 1

Mrs Alderman has just finished marking exam papers. She had 120 papers to mark in total. The paper is marked out of 150. In order to work out how well students are doing, she wants to put the data she has collected into a pie chart.

GRADE	A	B	C	D	E	F
FREQUENCY	10	15	60	20	10	5

For this task, you will need:

- A pencil
- A ruler
- A protractor

Put this data into a pie chart. The pie has been drawn for you.

QUESTION 2

Below is a dual bar chart showing the data from a survey about children's favourite activity. The results are recorded for boys and girls.

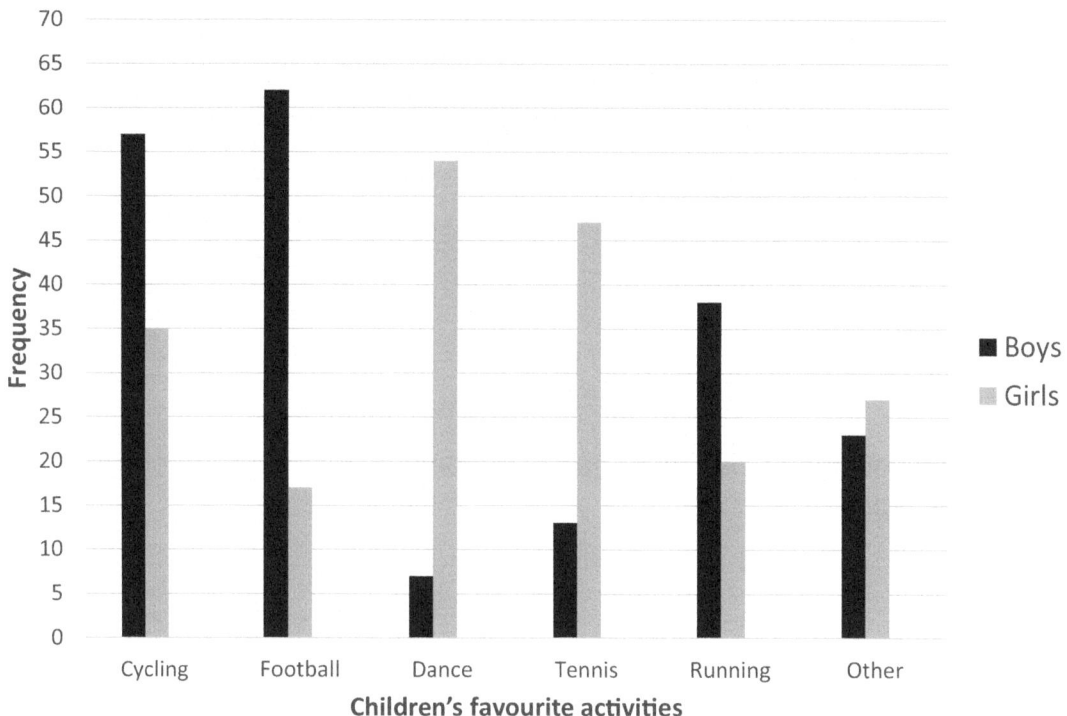

a) How many people took part in this survey?

b) What was the mean score for the number of people who choose football as their favourite activity?

c) How many more people choose cycling instead of tennis?

d) List three facts that you can state from the information provided.

1.

2.

3.

e) Why do you think a dual bar chart is the best choice of graph/chart to use for this type of data?

f) Circle whether the statement is true or false.

More girls preferred running than boys.	**TRUE / FALSE**
50 people chose a different activity listed.	**TRUE / FALSE**
There is a difference of 47 between boys and girls for dance.	**TRUE / FALSE**
Dance was the least popular amongst girls.	**TRUE / FALSE**

QUESTION 3

Below is a bar chart showing how students travelled to school.

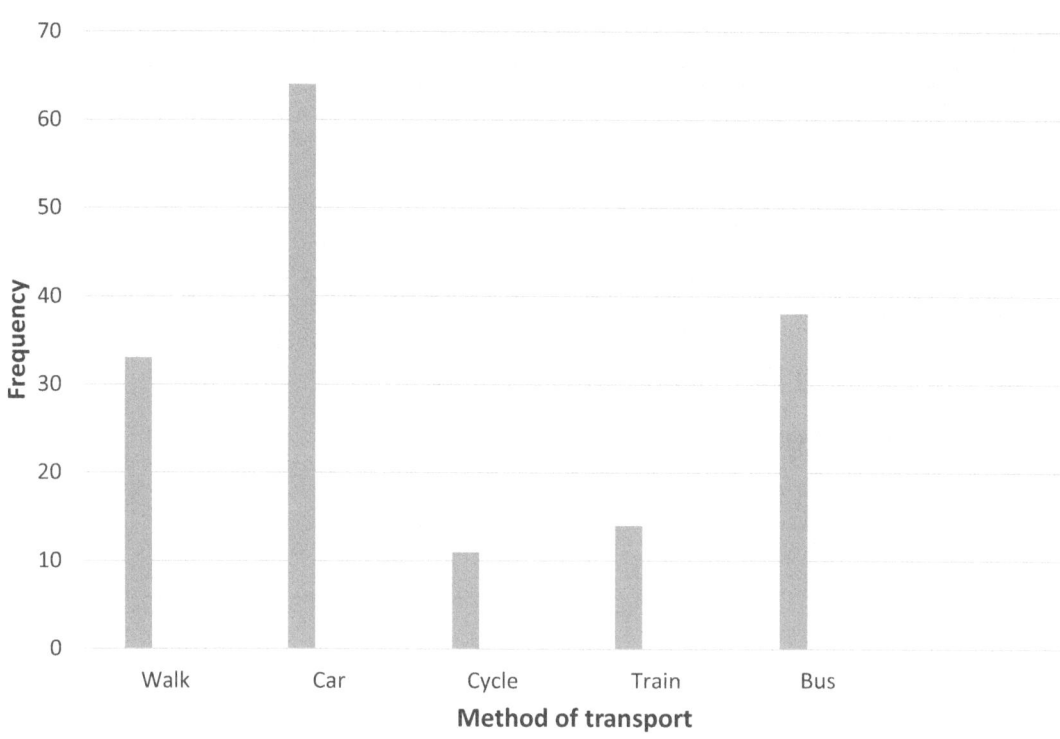

a) What is the modal method of transport?

b) How many people took part in the survey?

c) How many people travelled by public transport?

d) How many people travelled by transport which does not involve a large vehicle?

QUESTION 4

Below is a pie chart. It is yet to be filled in.

a) Using the information on the right-hand side, complete the pie chart.

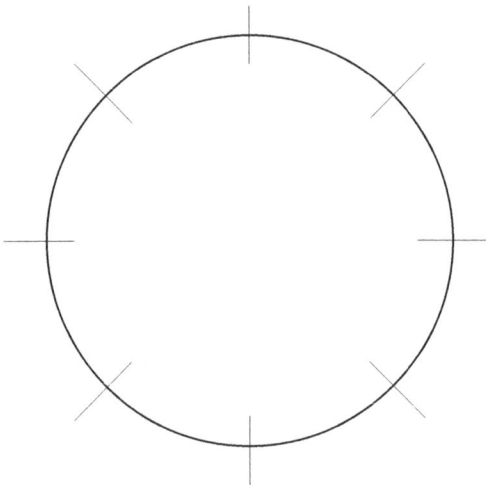

160 people took part in the survey.

85 people had brown eyes.

40 people had blue eyes.

5 people had green eyes.

30 people had hazel eyes.

b) Based on the information provided, what angle should the category 'blue eyes' be?

c) What percentage of the total number of people have green eyes? To the nearest whole number.

d) How many more people have blue eyes as opposed to hazel eyes?

QUESTION 5

The following pie chart shows children's favourite crisps flavour. The survey was of 180 children.

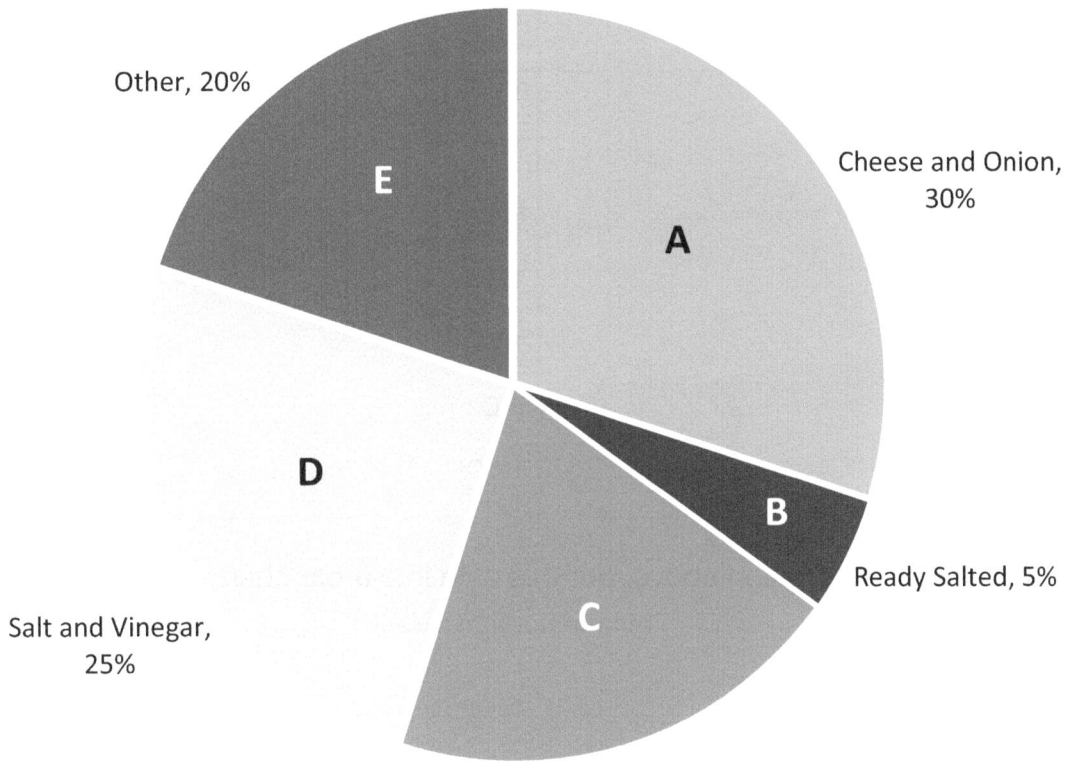

a) How many children chose salt and vinegar as their favourite crisps flavour?

b) What fraction of children preferred prawn cocktail crisps?

c) How many more people choose cheese and onion as opposed to ready salted?

QUESTION 6

Temperatures were recorded for a week. Each temperature was recorded at 12 noon every day. The results are as shown below.

DAY	TEMPERATURE
Monday	16°C
Tuesday	7°C
Wednesday	5°C
Thursday	12°C
Friday	10°C
Saturday	6°C
Sunday	15°C

a) Using the information above, put this data into a bar chart.

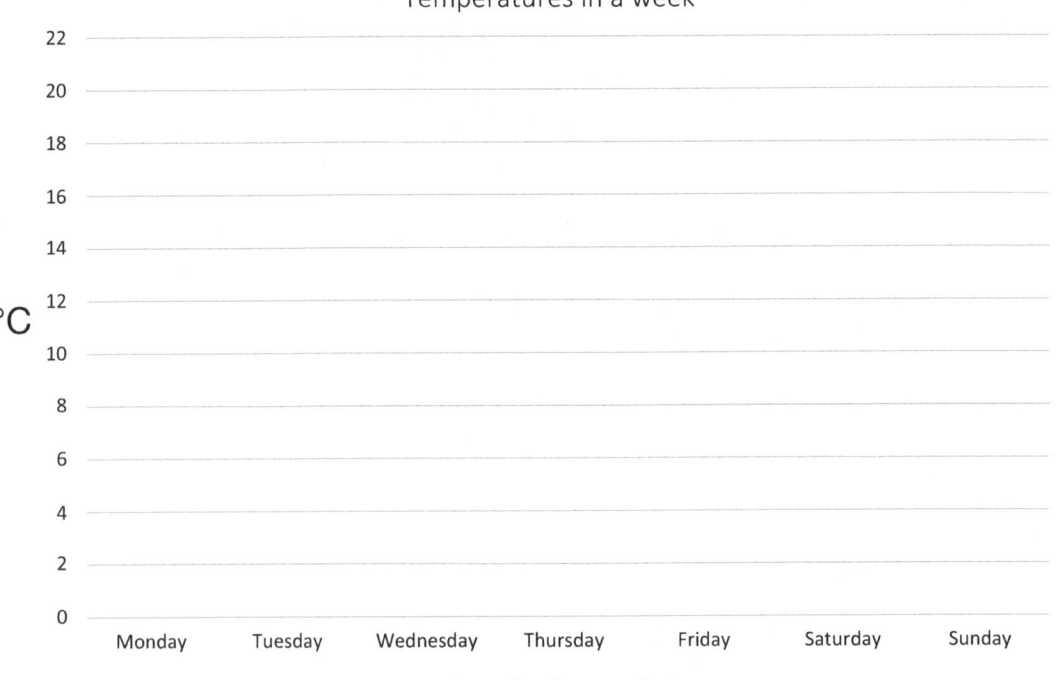

b) What is the range of temperatures recorded?

c) What is the mean temperature recorded? To two decimal places.

d) Results are recorded for the following week.

DAY	TEMPERATURE
Monday	13°C
Tuesday	15°C
Wednesday	12°C
Thursday	12°C
Friday	8°C
Saturday	10°C
Sunday	11°C

1) What is the difference in temperature recorded for Wednesday?

2) Which week was the coldest based on the overall mean temperature?

Answers

Q1.

Your answer should look something like this:

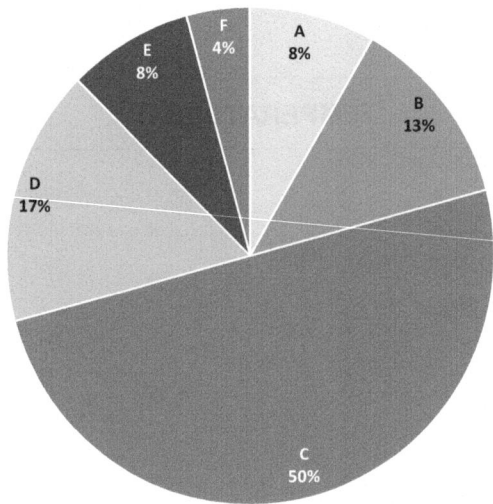

- A = 10/120 x 360 = 30°
- B = 15/120 x 360 = 45°
- C = 60/120 x 360 = 180°
- D = 20/120 x 360 = 60°
- E = 10/120 x 360 = 30°
- F = 5/120 x 360 = 15°

Q2.

a) 400
- Boys = 57 + 62 + 7 + 13 + 38 + 23 = 200
- Girls = 35 + 17 + 54 + 47 + 20 + 27 = 200
- Boys and girls = 200 + 200 = 400

b) 39.5
- 62 + 17 = 79
- 79 ÷ 2 = 39.5

BARS AND PIES 79

c) 32
- Cycling = 57 + 35 = 92
- Tennis = 13 + 47 = 60
- 92 − 60 = 32

d) *These facts can be anything that you can conclude from the data provided.

For example:

- 18 more boys preferred running compared to girls.
- Boys' least favourite activity was dance.
- The most popular sport amongst boys and girls was cycling.

e)
A dual bar chart is the best choice of chart to display this data because it allows you to compare the results from two categories. Not only does it show you the frequencies of choosing a particular activity, but you can also analyse the data in terms of gender, and therefore it allows you to draw comparisons.

f)
- More girls preferred running than boys. **FALSE**
- 50 people chose a different activity listed. **TRUE**
- There is a 47 difference between boys and girls for dance. **TRUE**
- Dance was the least popular amongst girls. **FALSE**

Q3.

a)
Car
- The mode (most frequent) means of transport is the car.

b)
160
- 33 + 64 + 11 + 14 + 38 = 160

c)

52

- Bus = 38
- Train = 14

d)

44

- Walk = 33
- Cycle = 11

Q4.

a)

Your answer should look something like this:

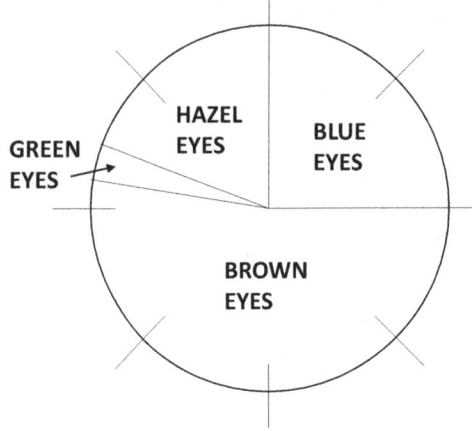

b)

90°

- The number of people who have blue eyes is 40.
- This is a quarter of the total number of people (160).
- The fact that it is ¼ (i.e. 25%) means that this will cover 25% of the circle.
- 25% of 360° is 90°.

c)

3%

- 5/360 x 100 = 3.125
- To the nearest whole number = 3%.

d)

10

- 40 − 30 = 10

Q5.

a)

45

- 180 (total number of children) ÷ 100 x 25% = 45

b)

1/5

- 180 (total number of children) ÷ 100 x 20% = 36
- 36/180 or 1/5

c)

45

- Cheese and Onion = 180 ÷ 100 x 30 = 54
- Ready Salted = 180 ÷ 100 x 5 = 9
- 54 − 9 = 45

Q6.

a)

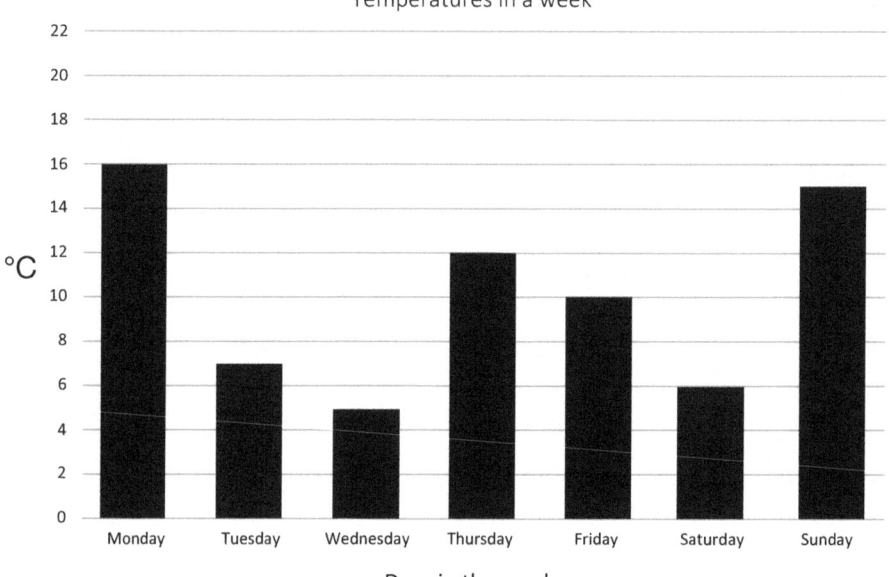

b)

11°C

- Range = highest – lowest = 16 – 5 = 11°C

c)

10.14°C

- 16 + 7 + 5 + 12 + 10 + 6 + 15 = 71
- 71 ÷ 7 = 10.14285…
- To two decimal places = 10.14°C

d)

(1) 7°C

- 12 – 5 = 7°C

(2) Week 1

- 16 + 7 + 5 + 12 + 10 + 6 + 15 = 71
- 71 ÷ 7 = 10.14285…
- To two decimal places = 10.14°C

- 13 + 15 + 12 + 12 + 8 + 10 + 11 = 81
- 81 ÷ 7 = 11.57142…
- To two decimal places = 11.57°C

So Week 1 was the coldest week.

HOW ARE YOU GETTING ON?

THE
REVISION
SERIES

SCATTER AND LINES

(Representing Data)

SCATTER GRAPHS

Understanding the correlation!

Scatter graphs are diagrams which analyse multiple sets of data.

They show the relationship between two variables, which makes it easier to analyse the data provided.

The link between the two variables is also called **CORRELATION**.

If the two variables are related in some way, you should be able to draw a **STRAIGHT LINE** through the middle of the points.

This straight line does not have to go through every single point on the scatter graph, but must pass most of the points closely.

This straight line is also known as '**THE LINE OF BEST FIT**'.

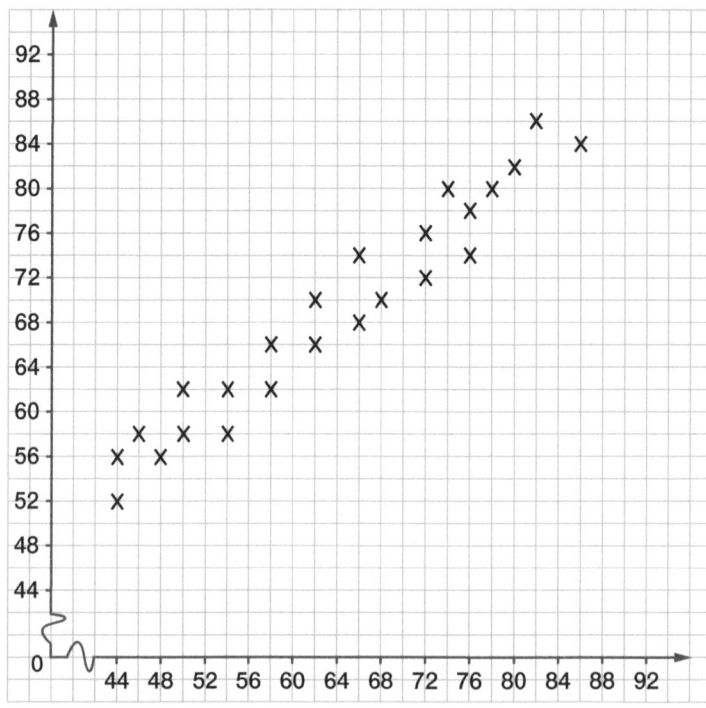

SCATTER AND LINES 87

THERE ARE 3 TYPES OF CORRELATION!

- Positive correlation
- Negative correlation
- No correlation

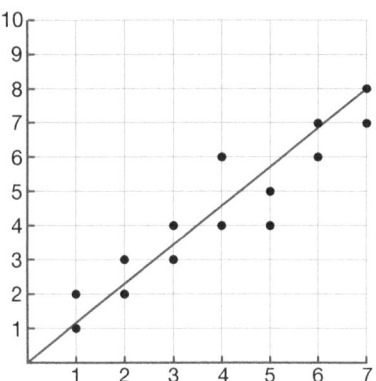

POSITIVE CORRELATION

The points must slant uphill (from left to right). This means that both variables either increase or decrease together.

You can draw a straight line through the plotted data. Dots need to be placed fairly evenly either side of the straight line.

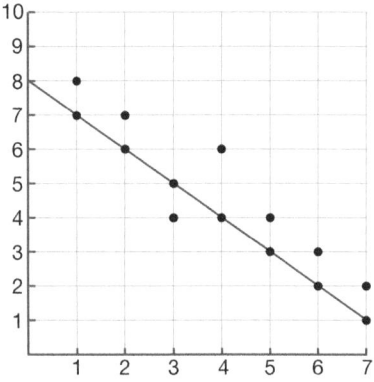

NEGATIVE CORRELATION

This means that the points slope downwards (from left to right). As one variable increases, the other decreases.

You can draw a line of best fit through the plotted data.

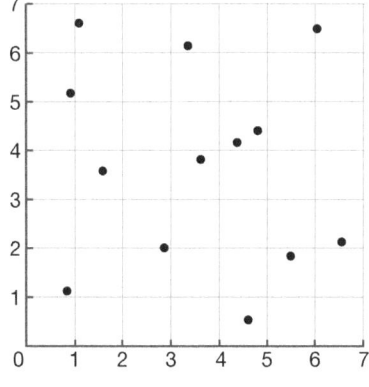

NO CORRELATION

No correlation means that the points are scattered all over the place, and therefore you are unable to draw a line of best fit.

This means that the two variables show no relation.

Each of these correlations can be **strong** or **weak**.

If the correlation is strong, that means that the plotted data is presented close together.

If the correlation is weak, that means that the plotted data is presented spread out.

STRONG POSITIVE CORRELATION

WEAK POSITIVE CORRELATION

STRONG NEGATIVE CORRELATION

WEAK NEGATIVE CORRELATION

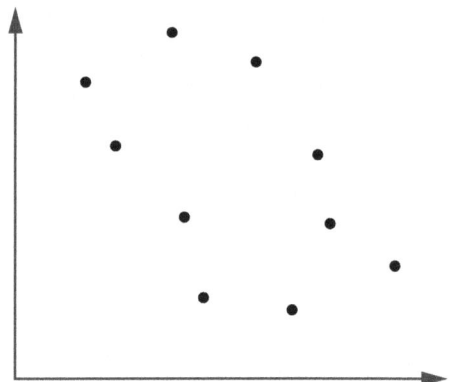

LINE GRAPHS

A line graph is used to represent data over a specific amount of time.

It is often used to show **TRENDS**.

Instead of using bars like a bar chart, a line graph uses lines by plotting on the points and drawing a line through each of these points.

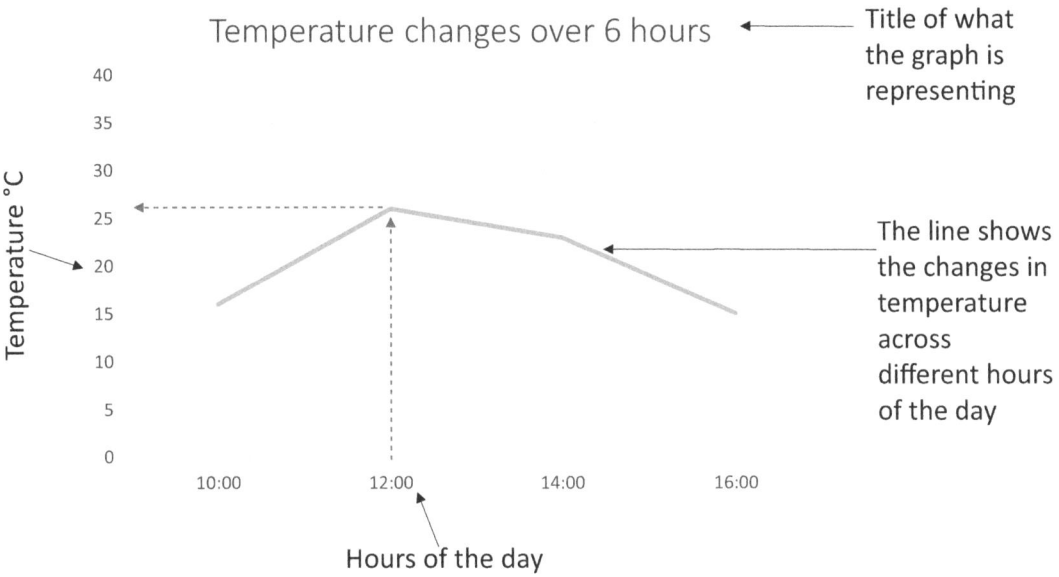

Work out the temperature at 12:00

Step 1 = draw an arrow from 12:00 all the way until you reach the line.
Step 2 = then read along that line and see what number it is.
Step 3 = the answer is 26 °C.

The ends of the line **DO NOT** have to join the axes.

QUESTION 1

Below is a line graph showing the amount of rainfall (in millimetres) across several hours of a day.

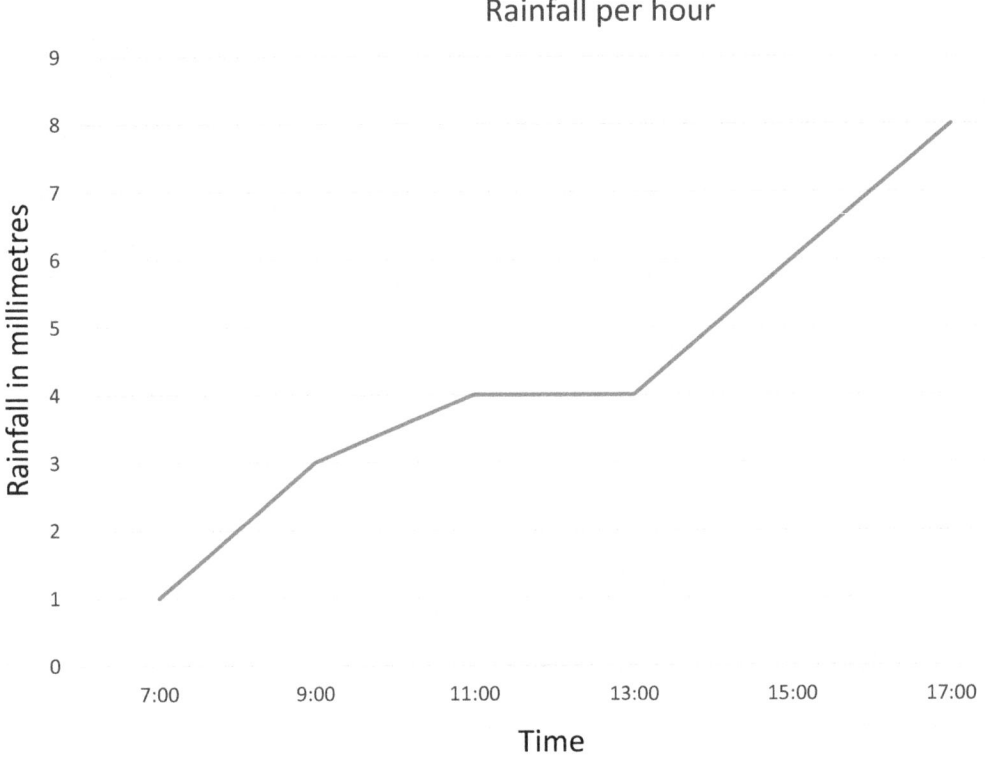

a) How many millimetres of rain fell at 16:00?

b) Between what times had 4 millimetres of rain fallen?

SCATTER AND LINES

QUESTION 2

The below table shows the results of 10 students' Maths and English scores. Both tests were out of 20.

English	12	18	17	5	9	11	10	18	19
Maths	19	10	4	16	10	14	16	18	20

a) Plot this data on the scatter graph below.

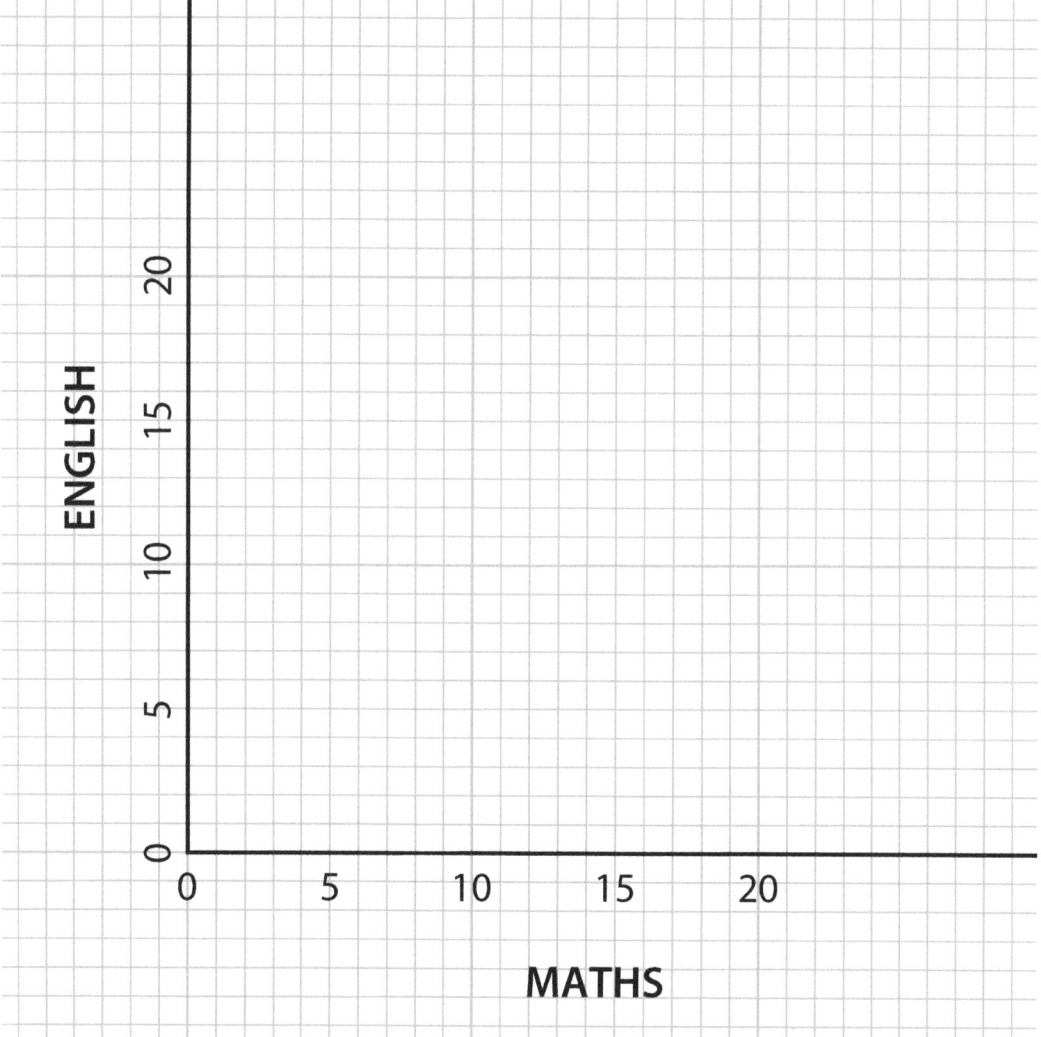

b) Draw a line (if applicable) of best fit through the data.

c) Is the data positive or negative, or does it show no correlation? If so, is it weak or strong? How can you tell?

_____

_____

_____

_____

QUESTION 3

Below is a blank graph.

> Begin at 0,0.
> In 10 minutes, he travels 6 km.
> In 20 minutes, he travels 18 km.
> In 30 minutes, he travels 42 km.
> In 40 minutes, he travels 60 km.
> In 50 minutes, he travels 72 km.
> In 60 minutes, he travels 94 km.

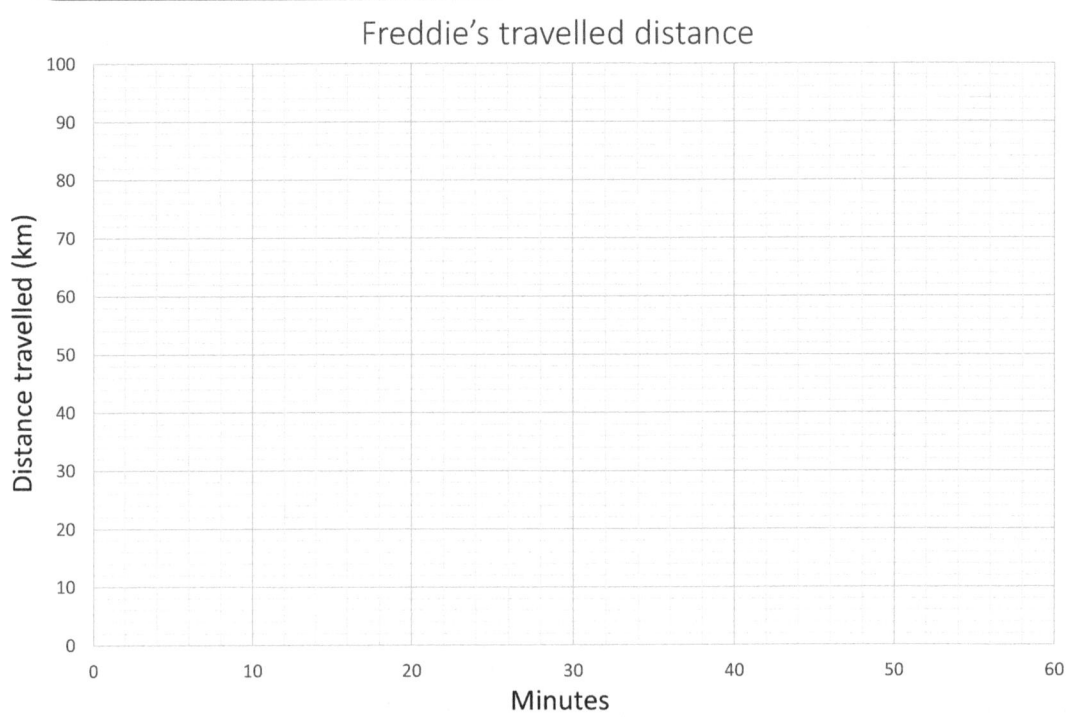

a) Plot the data above on the graph.

b) How many minutes does it take to travel 30 kilometres?

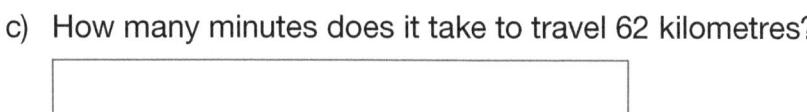

c) How many minutes does it take to travel 62 kilometres?

QUESTION 4

Below is a scatter graph.

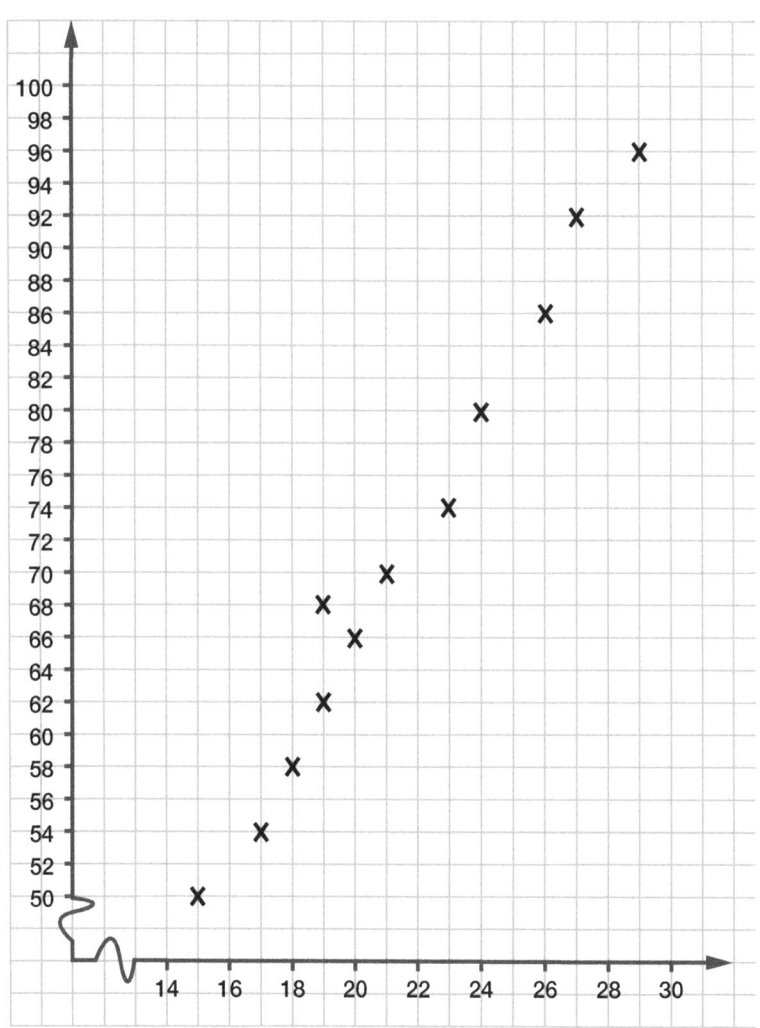

a) You should have noticed that there is a jagged line where the *y* and *x* axis meet. This is known as a **broken scale**.

Why do you think the graph uses this?

_____

_____

_____

b) Tick which type of correlation this graph shows.

Positive correlation ☐

Negative correlation ☐

No correlation ☐

How do you know this? ☐

_____

_____

_____

c) Draw a line of best fit through the plotted data.

SCATTER AND LINES

QUESTION 5

Study the diagrams below.

a) Which diagram/s show a positive correlation? Tick all that apply.

Diagram A

Diagram B

Diagram C

Diagram D

Diagram E

b) Which diagram do you think most shows the relationship between temperature and the number of ice lollies sold?

Diagram A ☐

Diagram B ☐

Diagram C ☐

Diagram D ☐

Diagram E ☐

c) Which diagram/s show the relationship between height and weight?

Diagram A ☐

Diagram B ☐

Diagram C ☐

Diagram D ☐

Diagram E ☐

d) Which diagram shows a moderate positive correlation?

   Diagram A ☐

   Diagram B ☐

   Diagram C ☐

   Diagram D ☐

   Diagram E ☐

e) Which diagram/s show no correlation?

   Diagram A ☐

   Diagram B ☐

   Diagram C ☐

   Diagram D ☐

   Diagram E ☐

f) Using your answer to part e), can you think of two examples of what the graph data could be representing.

1. _____

2. _____

Answers

Q1.

a) 7 mm

(Find the middle between 15:00 and 17:00 – this will give you 16:00. You should notice that the line on the graph represents 7 mm for this hour.)

b) 11:00 – 13:00

(Between these hours, the line on the graph remains on 4 mm.)

Q2.

a)

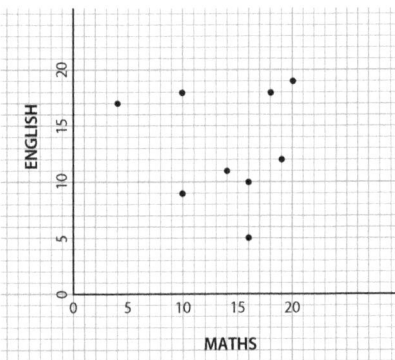

b)

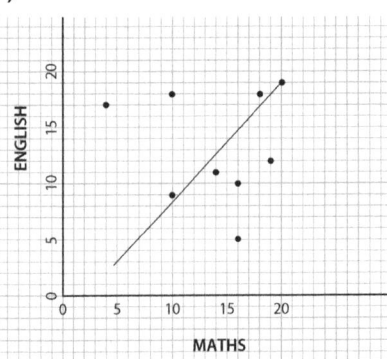

SCATTER AND LINES

c) The line of best fit shows a weak positive correlation between the data. Generally, when someone scores highly in English, they also score highly in Maths. Although, this is not always the case, many of the results do show a weak relationship between test scores.

Q3.

a)

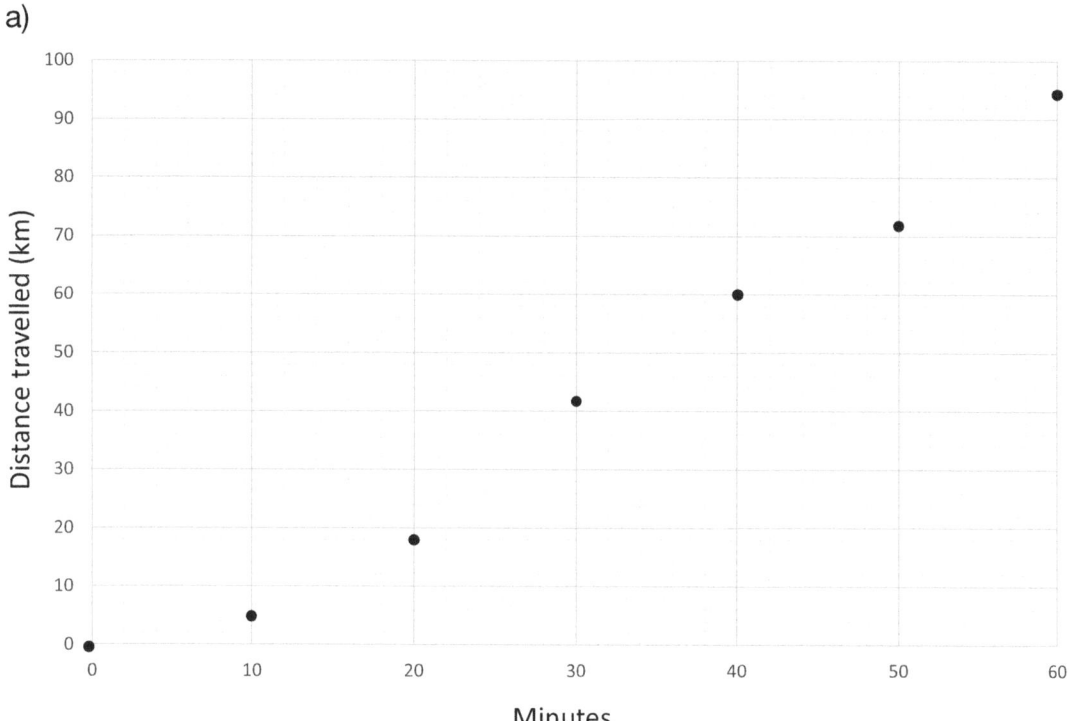

b) 25 minutes

(The easiest way is to work this out is to draw lines between the dots, and then find where the line goes through 30 kilometres.)

c) 42 minutes

(The easiest way is to work this out is to draw lines between the dots, and then find where the line goes through 30 kilometres.)

Q4.

a) The graph uses a broken scale because it demonstrates that the graph does not begin with the number '0'. Instead, on the *y* axis it begins with the number '50', and on the *x* axis it begins with the number '14'.

b) The graph shows a **positive correlation**. You know this because the plotted data is increasing. In other words, if the number is high for the *y* axis, then the number is also high on the *x* axis.

c)

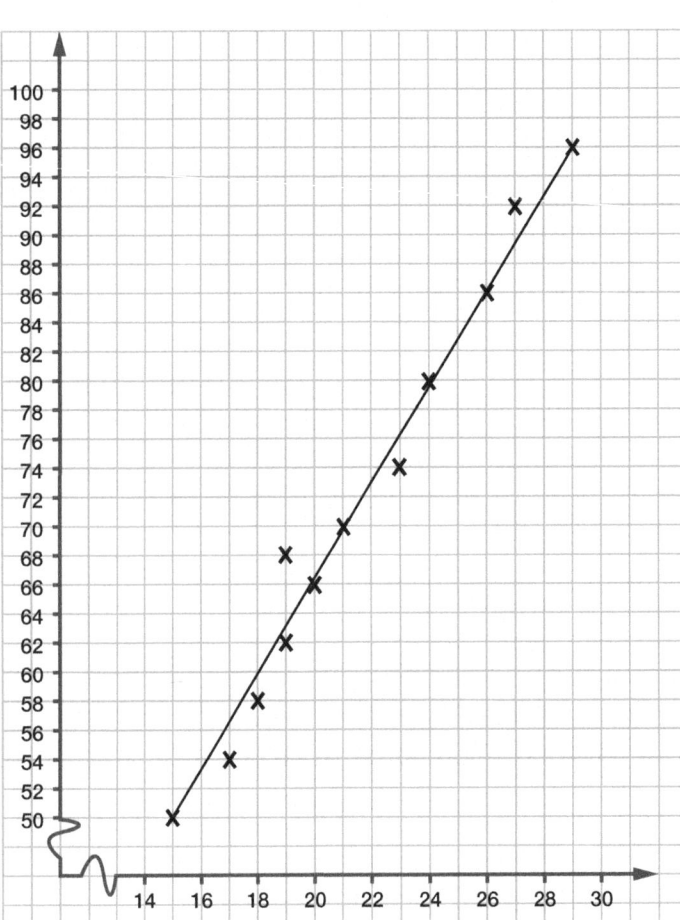

Q5.

a) Diagrams D and E
b) Diagram D
c) Diagram E
d) Diagram E
e) Diagrams B and C
f) *These can be any two components that would show no relationship.

<u>For example:</u>
- Height and the way people travel to school.
- Test scores and the time taken to run 100 meters.

THE
REVISION
SERIES

FREQUENCIES AND TALLIES

(Representing Data)

FREQUENCY TABLES

Frequency basically means:

'THE NUMBER OF TIMES SOMETHING OCCURS'.

Using tables is a great way to keep track of data collected.

You will normally have a category row, a tally row (optional), and a frequency row.

This will allow you to quickly see how many are in each category.

TRANSPORT	FREQUENCY
Car	22
Train	13
Bus	38
Walk	8
Cycle	17

CATEGORIES — HOW MANY IN EACH CATEGORY

After collecting and recording the data, you are then able to display that data in a graph or chart, such as a **BAR CHART**!

FREQUENCIES AND TALLIES

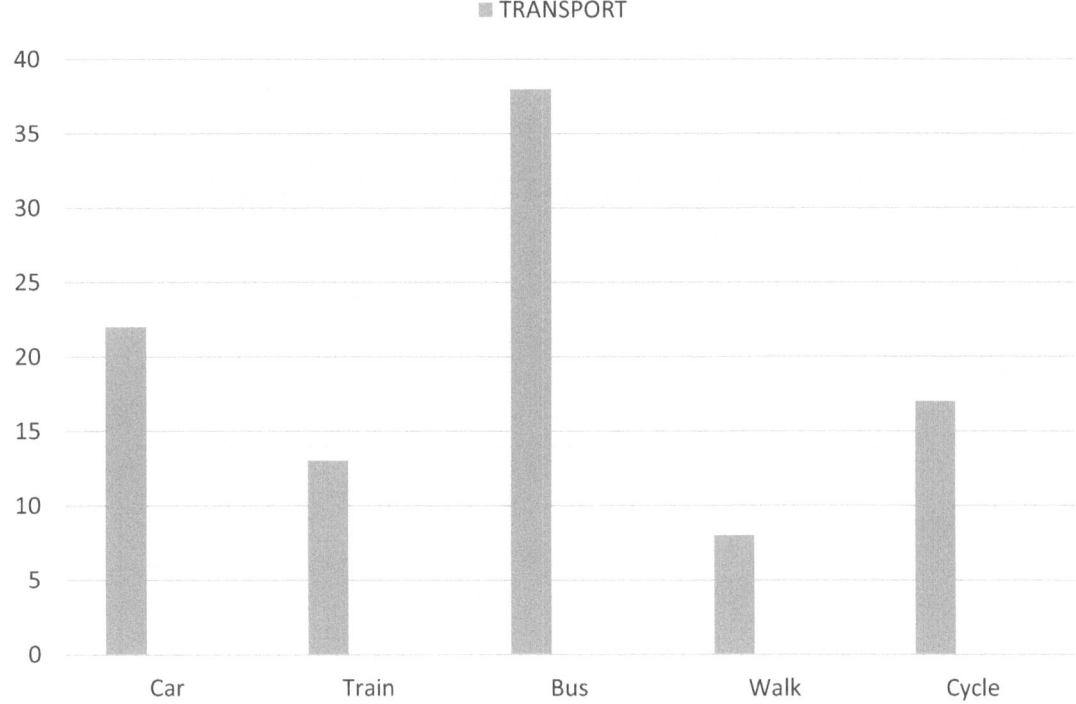

Sometimes, instead of having just individual categories, you will have what is called **GROUPED FREQUENCIES**.

Group frequencies is data that can be put into classes.

INEQUALITIES often occur in data which doesn't always deal with whole numbers.

INEQUALITIES
The number 5 would be recorded in the top row, but the number 5.1 would be recorded in the second row.

HEIGHT	FREQUENCY
$0 < h \leq 5$	4
$5 < h \leq 10$	10
$10 < h \leq 15$	2
$15 < h \leq 20$	5

$\leq$
This sign means 'equal to or less than'.

With the information you have collected, you are able to put that data into a frequency bar chart.

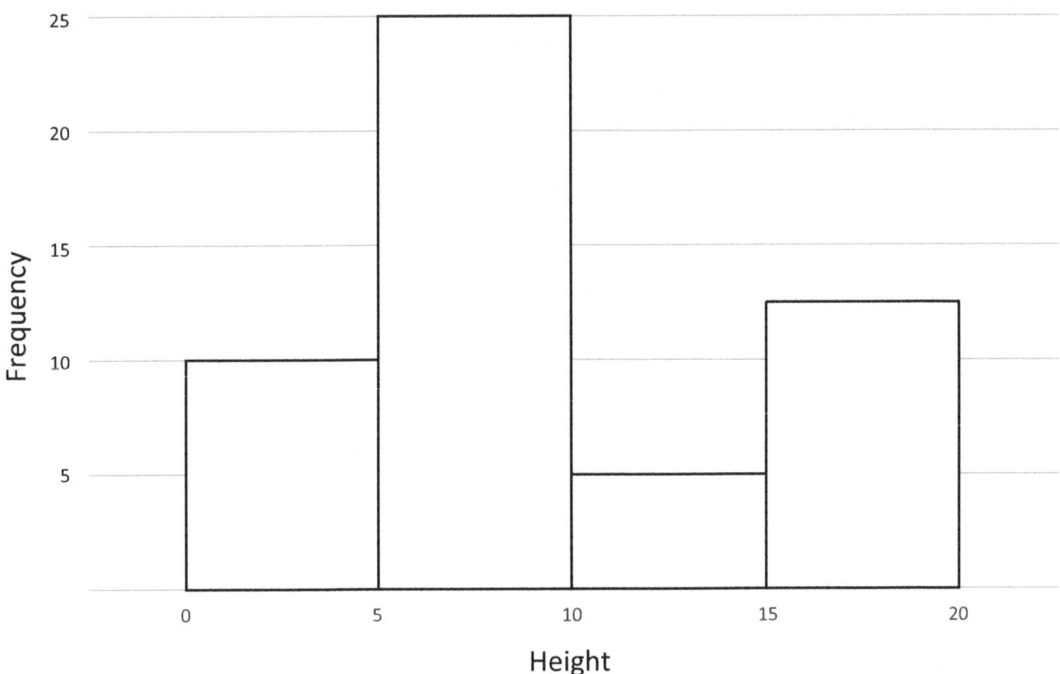

See how the bars in this chart have no gaps.

This is because the groups of classes have no gaps. In simpler terms, because the data deals with whole numbers and inequalities, there cannot be any gaps between the bars, as the data is flowing straight from one class to another.

For more information on drawing bar charts, please check out the chapter 'Bars and Pies' on pages 63 – 83.

FREQUENCIES AND TALLIES

Instead of drawing bar charts, you can also use **FREQUENCY POLYGONS**.

However, this is slightly trickier and you must remember this rule:

YOU MUST ALWAYS PLOT YOUR DATA AT THE MID-INTERVAL VALUE OF A CLASS/CATEGORY.

HOW TO WORK OUT THE MID-INTERVAL POINT OF A SET OF DATA:

- In your table, you should have your categories and frequencies.
- To work out the mid-interval value, you need to add the upper and lower limits, and then divide that by 2.

The best way for you to understand this more clearly is via example.

EXAMPLE

HEIGHT	$0 \leq h < 5$	$5 \leq h < 10$	$10 \leq h < 15$	$15 \leq h < 20$
Frequency	4	10	2	5
Mid-interval value	2.5	7.5	12.5	17.5

- $0 + 5 = 5$ $5 \div 2 = 2.5$
- $5 + 10 = 15$ $15 \div 2 = 7.5$
- $10 + 15 = 25$ $25 \div 2 = 12.5$
- $15 + 20 = 35$ $35 \div 2 = 17.5$

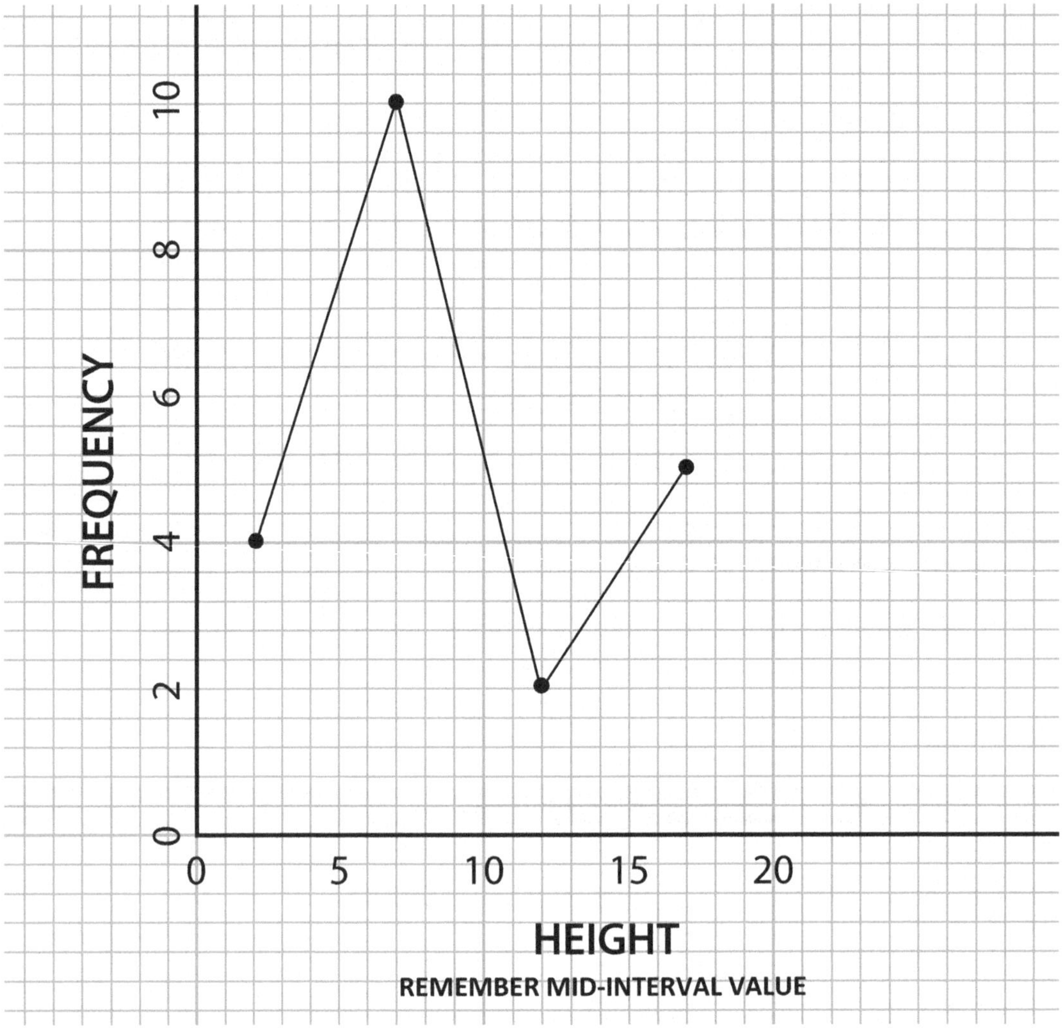

(Frequency polygon graph showing Frequency vs Height, with points plotted at approximately (2,4), (7,10), (12,2), (17,5))

HEIGHT

REMEMBER MID-INTERVAL VALUE

ACTIVITY TIME!

Draw a frequency bar chart and a frequency polygon for the data below.

WEIGHT	0 ≤ h < 10	10 ≤ h < 20	20 ≤ h < 30	30 ≤ h < 40
Frequency	18	6	13	10
Mid-interval value				

FREQUENCIES AND TALLIES

WORKING OUT AVERAGES FROM FREQUENCY TABLES

Frequency tables are very handy, because they allow you to work out **AVERAGES**.

The following words should be at the forefront of your mind:

- Mean
- Mode
- Median
- Range

Go back to the chapter entitled 'Mean. Mode, Median and Range' (pages 43 – 54) for more information.

TO WORK OUT THE MODE
(Mode = Most)

- The frequency with the most number of pets is 17 for '1 pet'.
- So the mode is 1.

No. of pets	FREQUENCY
0	16
1	17
2	16
3	8
4	4
5	2

TO WORK OUT THE RANGE
(Difference between highest and lowest)

- The highest number of sweets is 5 and the lowest number of sweets is 0.
- So, 5 – 0 = 5.

No. of sweets	FREQUENCY
0	16
1	8
2	3
3	7
4	5
5	3

TO WORK OUT THE MEAN
Add up the values of 'no. of sweets x frequency' and then divide it by how many people were asked.

- So, the mean is:

  $\frac{70}{42} = 1.67$

No. of sweets	FREQUENCY	No. of sweets x frequency
0	16	0
1	8	8
2	3	6
3	7	21
4	5	20
5	3	15
TOTAL	42	70

TO WORK OUT THE MEDIAN
(Median = Middle)

The total frequency is 42. Halfway between this is 21. So you are trying to find the 21st value.

There are a total of 16 people in the first category (0). There are 8 people in the second category (1). That means (16 + 8 = 24). So you know that the 21st value will be in the second category.

So the median is 1.

No. of pets	FREQUENCY
0	16
1	17
2	16
3	8
4	4
5	2

ACTIVITY TIME!

Can you work out the mode, mean, median and range from this set of data?

No. of books	FREQUENCY
0	28
1	20
2	8
3	28
4	7
5	11
6	22

FREQUENCIES AND TALLIES

TALLIES

TALLY CHARTS are all about keeping count!

Frequency tables often use tallies to keep track of who chooses what category, before all of the data is added together. The tally part to a frequency graph is often left off recorded data (you can finalise the tallies with a simple 'frequency total'.

Take a look at the below example for a better idea of what I mean by tally charts!

Tally marks will look like this:

1   2   3   4   5

Once you get to 4, the next tally mark will cross off the 4 marks (to make 5). This makes it easier to count the totals.

You can record this information using a tally and frequency graph.

Colours	Tally	Frequency
Pink	|||| |||| |||| |||	18
Blue	|||| ||||	10
Red	|||| ||||	9
Orange	|||| ||	7
Green	|||| |||| ||	12

Remember, **FREQUENCY** is another word for **TOTAL**.

Question Time!

QUESTION 1

Below is a list of how 24 children travel to school.

a) Use the data below and organise it in the tally and frequency diagram below. <u>The first tally has been done for you.</u>

Walk Cycle Walk Bus Bus Car Walk Train Taxi Car Walk Bus
Bus Walk Car Car Car Taxi Train Walk Walk Bus Bus Car

Transport	Tally	Frequency
Walk	|	
Bus		
Car		
Train		
Cycle		
Taxi		
TOTAL	24	24

b) What is the modal value for the way children travelled to school?

FREQUENCIES AND TALLIES

QUESTION 2

The table shows information about the lengths (in centimetres) of 20 snakes.

LENGTH (cm)	0 < l ≤ 10	10 < l ≤ 20	20 < l ≤ 30	30 < l ≤ 40	40 < l ≤ 50
Frequency	5	8	3	2	2
Mid-interval value					
Frequency x mid-interval value					

a) Draw a frequency polygon using the data above.

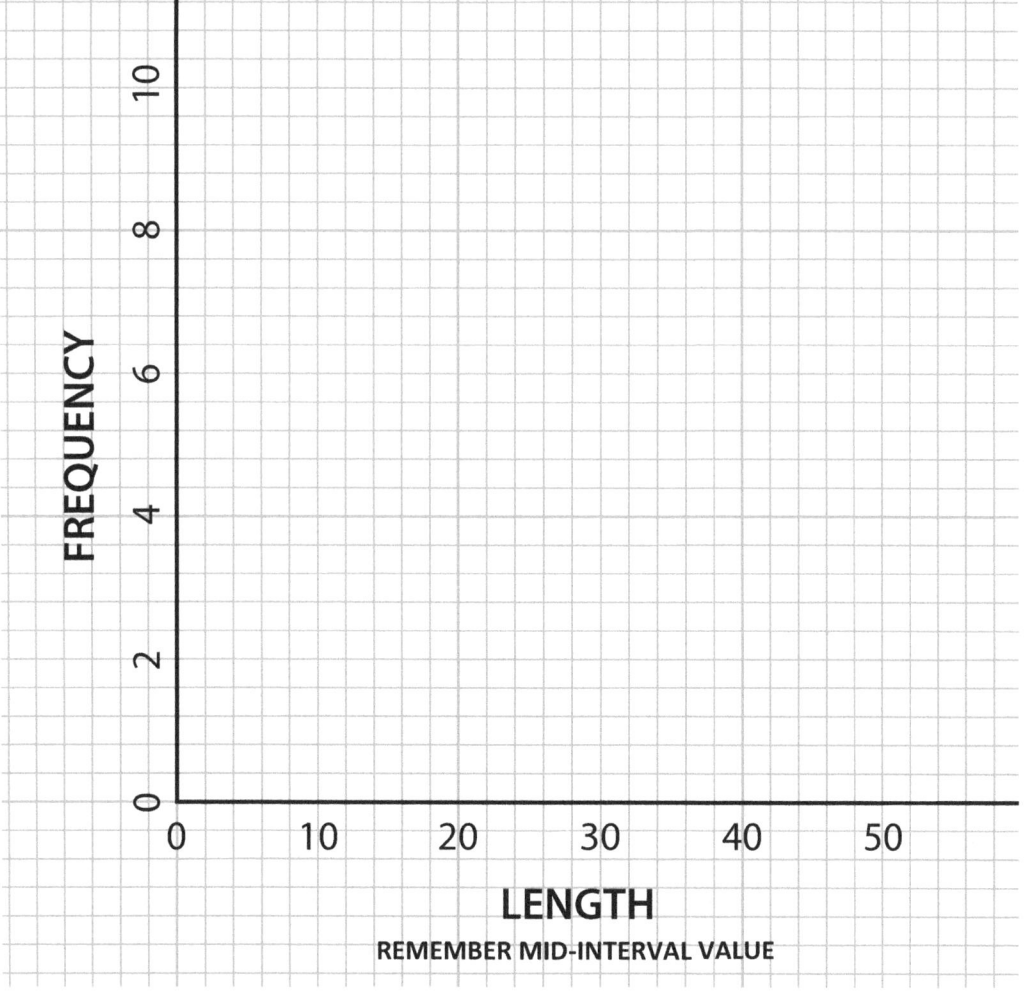

REMEMBER MID-INTERVAL VALUE

b) What length was the most frequent?

c) What does the ≤ sign mean?

d) Write down the frequency containing the median.

FREQUENCIES AND TALLIES   115

QUESTION 3

Below is a survey of 150 people and their favourite fruit choices.

a) Complete the tally chart below using the information provided. <u>The first one has been done for you.</u>

> The survey is of 150 people and their favourite fruit.
> ~~20% of the total people said their favourite fruit was **strawberries**.~~
> 10% of the total people said their favourite fruit was **oranges**.
> 4 people chose **kiwis** as their favourite fruit.
> 8 people chose **pears** as their favourite fruit.
> 2/5 of people chose **apples** as their favourite fruit.
> 1/6 of people chose **bananas** as their favourite fruit.
> The rest chose **raspberries** as their fruit.

Fruit	Tally	Frequency
Apples		
Bananas		
Strawberries	ЖЖ ЖЖ ЖЖ ЖЖ ЖЖ ЖЖ	30
Kiwis		
Oranges		
Pears		
Raspberries		

b) Calculate the range for this set of data.

c) Draw your own bar chart in the space provided to represent this data. Don't forget to label the axes.

FREQUENCIES AND TALLIES

QUESTION 4

The following table shows the number of cars that entered a local car park.

Number of cars	Frequency	No. of cars x frequency
0	3	
1	11	
3	12	
4	24	
5	24	
6	8	

a) Calculate the mode frequency.

b) Calculate the range frequency.

c) Calculate the median frequency.

Answers

Q1.

a)

Transport	Tally	Frequency
Walk	ⅠⅠⅠⅠ ⅠⅠ	7
Bus	ⅠⅠⅠⅠ Ⅰ	6
Car	ⅠⅠⅠⅠ Ⅰ	6
Train	ⅠⅠ	2
Cycle	Ⅰ	1
Taxi	ⅠⅠ	2
TOTAL	24	24

b) Walk

(The frequency for walking is '7'. No other category has a larger frequency.)

Q2.

a)

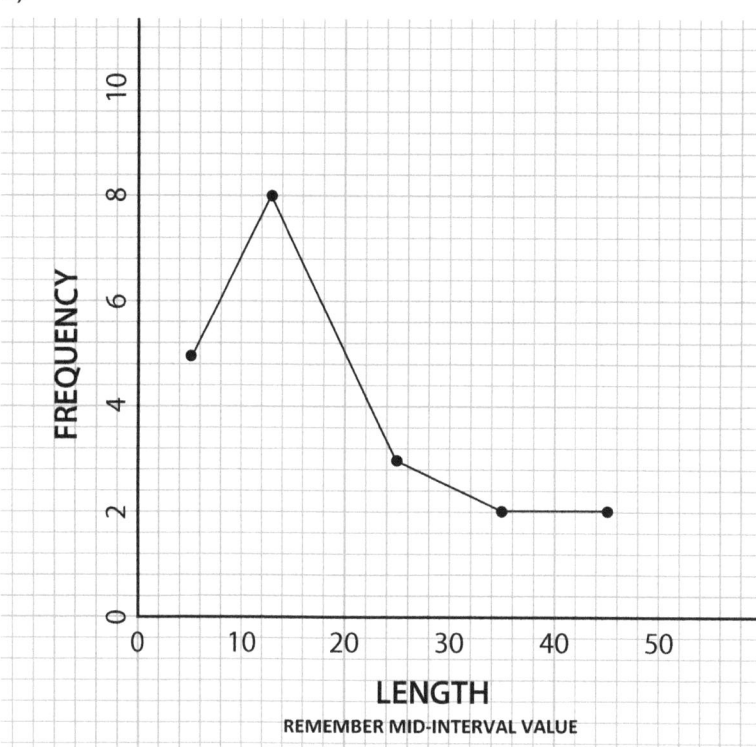

REMEMBER MID-INTERVAL VALUE

b) The most frequent length was $10 < l \leq 20$

c) The $\leq$ sign means equal to or less than.

d) The median value is $10 < l \leq 20$

(There are 20 values in total, which means 10 is the middle number. So the second column would contain this value.)

Q3.

a)

Fruit	Tally	Frequency
Apples	|||| |||| |||| |||| |||| |||| |||| |||| |||| |||| |||| ||||	60
Bananas	|||| |||| |||| |||| ||||	25
Strawberries	|||| |||| |||| |||| |||| ||||	30
Kiwis	||||	4
Oranges	|||| |||| ||||	15
Pears	|||| |||	8
Raspberries	|||| |||	8

b) 56

(Highest value subtract the lowest value = 60 – 4 = 56)

c) Your answer should look something like this:

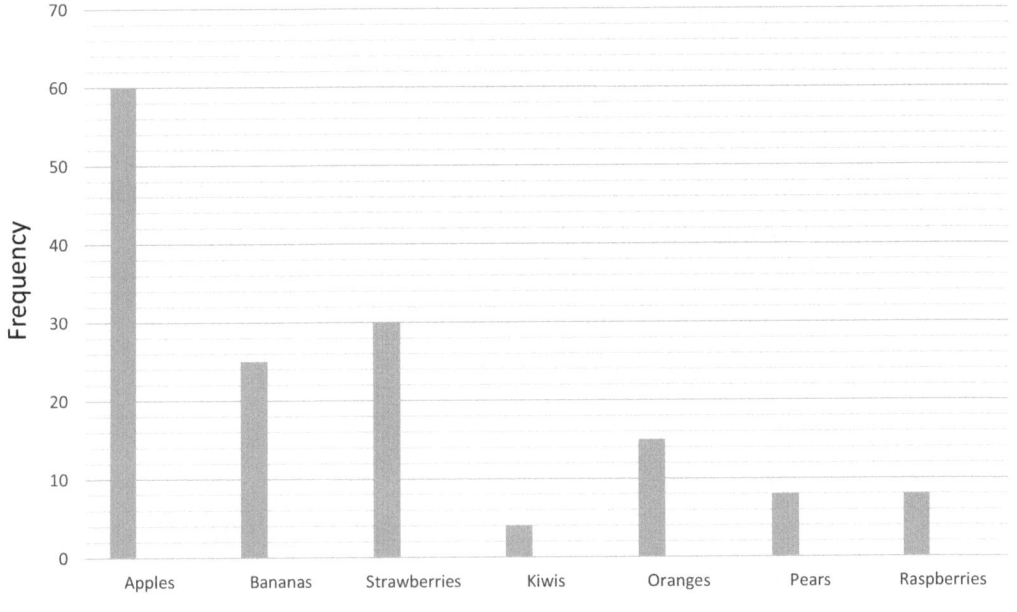

Q4.

a) 4 and 5 cars

(Both these categories have the value 24.)

b) 6

(Highest value subtract the lowest number of cars = 6 – 0 = 0)

c) 4

(Frequency total is 82. The middle number is 41. This number would occur in the fourth category (number of cars 4). So therefore the median is 4.)

| **HOW ARE YOU GETTING ON?** |

THE
REVISION
SERIES

PICTOGRAMS AND OTHER USEFUL DIAGRAMS

(Representing Data)

PICTOGRAMS

Pictograms use PICTURES to represent data.

In order for a pictogram to work, you must have a **KEY**.

EXAMPLE

Five people counted the number of balloons they were able to pop in 30 seconds. Here are their results.

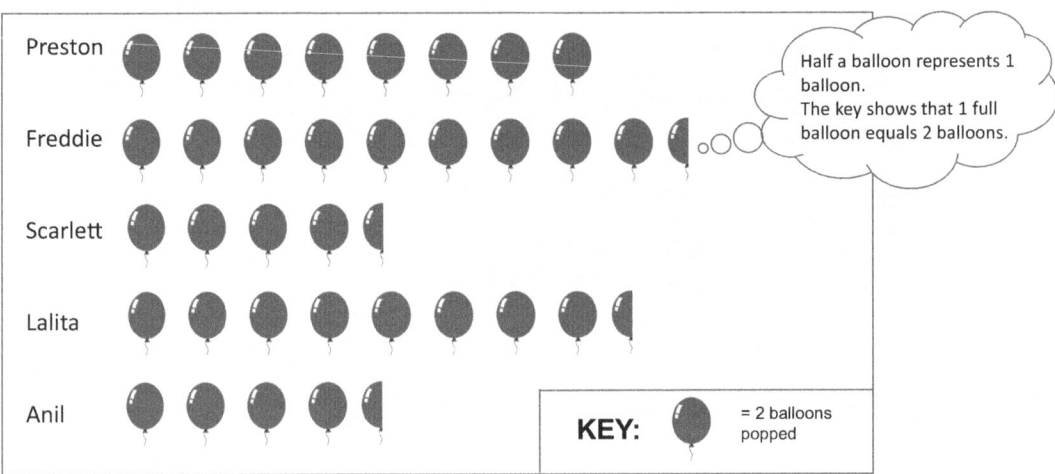

From the key, we can see that 1 picture of a balloon represents **2** balloons.

So, half a balloon represents **1** balloon.

ACTIVITY TIME!

Can you work out how many balloons each person popped?

PICTOGRAMS AND OTHER USEFUL DIAGRAMS

STEM AND LEAF DIAGRAMS

Stem and Leaf Diagrams work similarly to a tally!

In order for a pictogram to work, you must have a **KEY**.

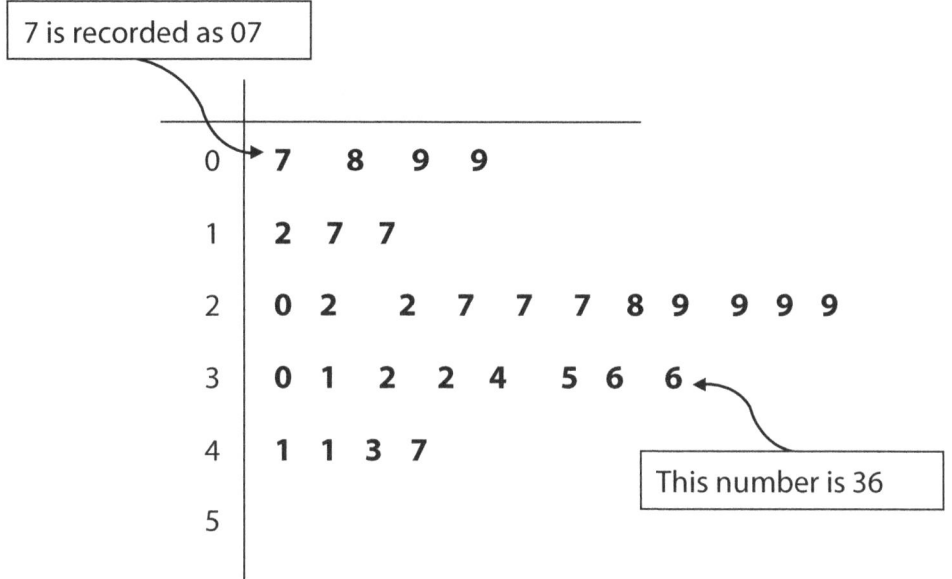

Stem and leaf diagrams act as a way of handling data. These become particularly useful when dealing with large sums of data.

They are also helpful ways to work out the **mean**, **mode**, **median** and **range**.

CARROLL DIAGRAMS

Carroll diagrams are a useful way of sorting out information and arranging the data under the correct headings.

The use of Carroll diagrams allows you to **categorise** your data under specific headings.

5 9 27 35 15 10 18 54 36 30 20

	Multiples of 5	Multiples of 9
ODD	5, 15, 35	9, 27
EVEN	10, 30, 20	36, 54, 18

TOP TIP!

Cross off the numbers as you go. By crossing the numbers off as you go, this will make it easier to know which numbers you have done, and which ones you still have to do.

PICTOGRAMS AND OTHER USEFUL DIAGRAMS

VENN DIAGRAMS

Similar to Carroll diagrams, Venn diagrams are another way of categorising data by placing them under the correct headings.

The main difference between a Carroll diagram and a Venn diagram is that a Venn diagram has a part that overlaps, which means data can overlap with multiple categories.

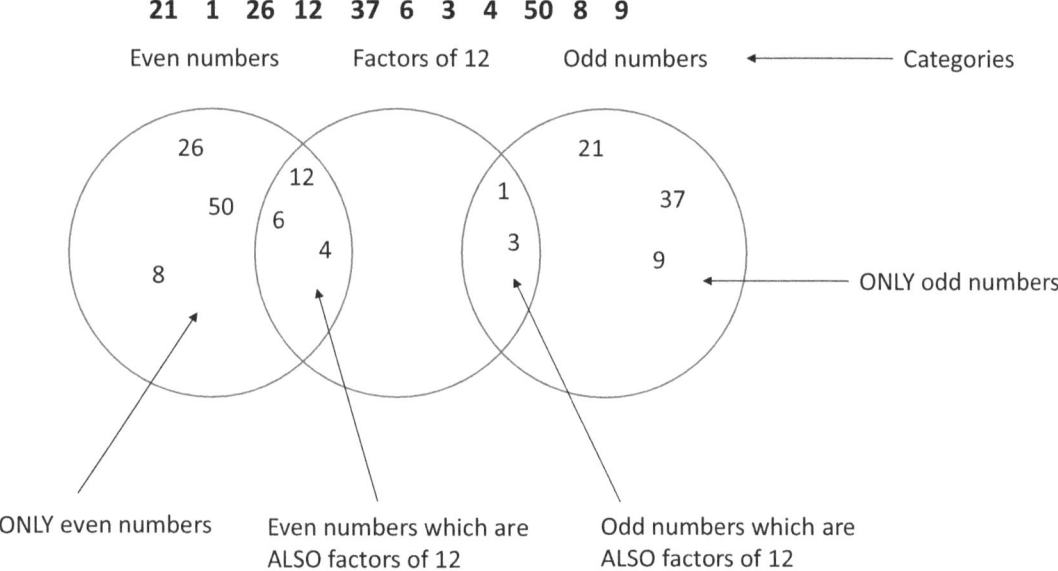

TOP TIP!

Be careful when placing the numbers under categories. Does the number apply to more than one category?

Question Time!

QUESTION 1

A receptionist records the number of phone calls she has to take per day. Her results are recorded for 30 days.

Her results are recorded using the stem and leaf diagram below.

KEY: 1|1 represents 11 phone calls

```
0 | 3 3 4 6 6 7 7 9 9 9
1 | 0 1 1 2 2 2 4 7 8 8 8 9
2 | 0 0 2 2 4 5 6 6
```

a) Work out the range.

b) Work out the mode.

c) Calculate the mean.

d) Work out the median.

PICTOGRAMS AND OTHER USEFUL DIAGRAMS

QUESTION 2

The pictogram below shows how many shooting stars Andy saw across 12 months.

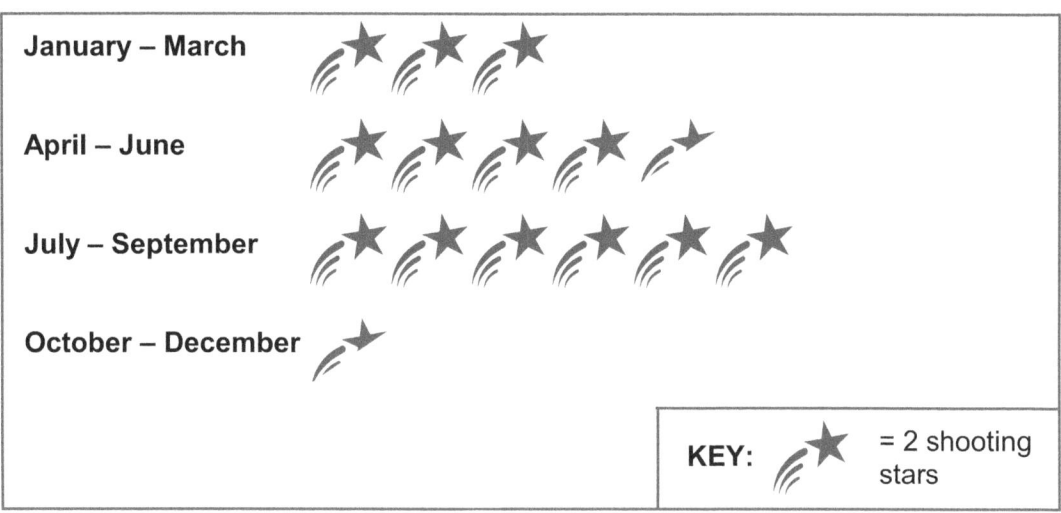

a) How many shooting stars did Andy see between April and June?

b) On average, how many shooting stars did Andy see per month, between January and March?

c) How many shooting stars did Andy see altogether?

d) From April to June and July to September, how many shooting stars were seen?

QUESTION 3

Put the following data into the Carroll diagram below.

26 2 42 17 9 11 90 31 49 7 55

	Even	Odd
Prime Numbers		
Not Prime		

QUESTION 4

Below is a Venn diagram. Using the data provided, fill in the Venn diagram.

3 15 14 21 35 28 5 7

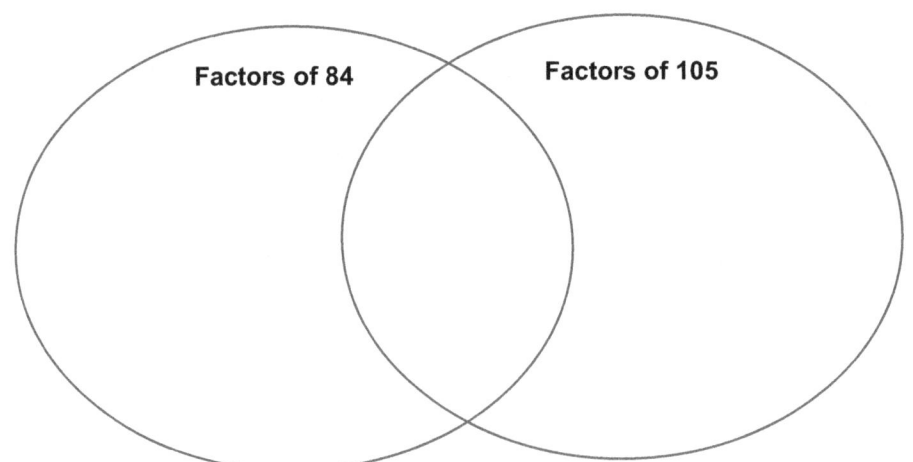

PICTOGRAMS AND OTHER USEFUL DIAGRAMS

QUESTION 5

a) Complete the pictogram using the data provided.

Favourite Ice Cream Flavour	Number of Children
Vanilla	9
Chocolate	14
Strawberry	4
Mint Chocolate	12
Rocky Road	2
Raspberry	7

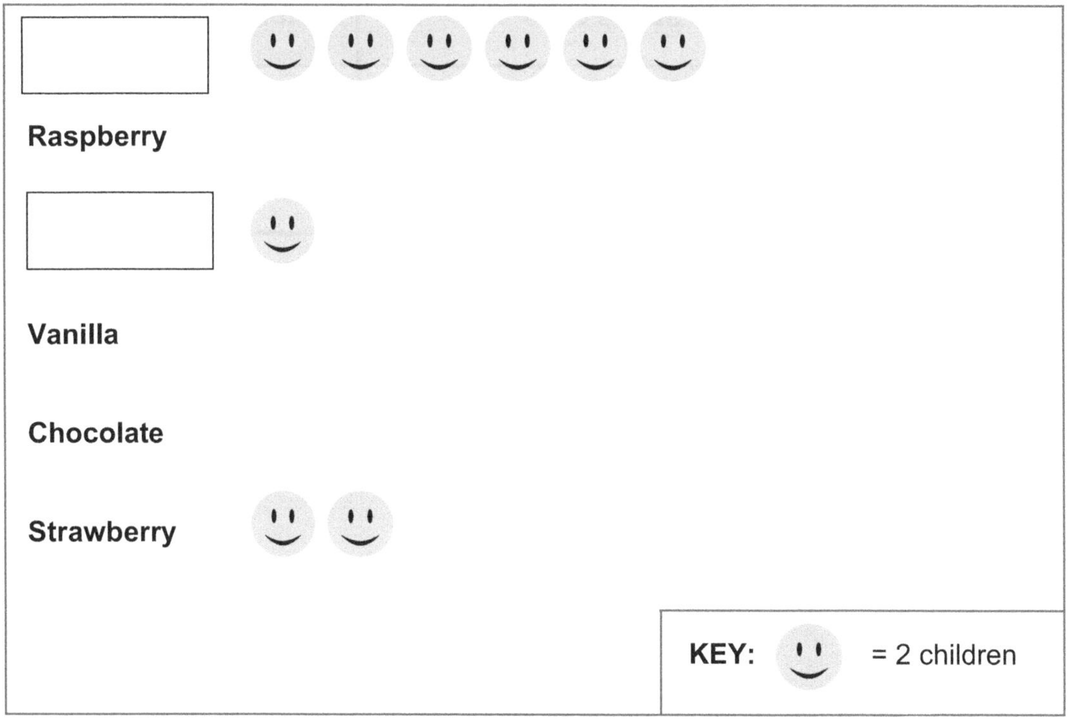

Raspberry ☺ ☺ ☺ ☺ ☺ ☺

Vanilla ☺

Chocolate

Strawberry ☺ ☺

KEY: ☺ = 2 children

b) How many people took part in this survey?

c) Which flavour is the second most popular?

QUESTION 6

Using the numbers listed below, place them in the correct part of the Carroll diagram.

8   5   6   18   10   12   20   9

	Factors of 36	Factors of 40
Numbers between 1 - 10		
Numbers between 11 - 20		

QUESTION 7

Below is a Venn diagram showing what children had in their lunchboxes.

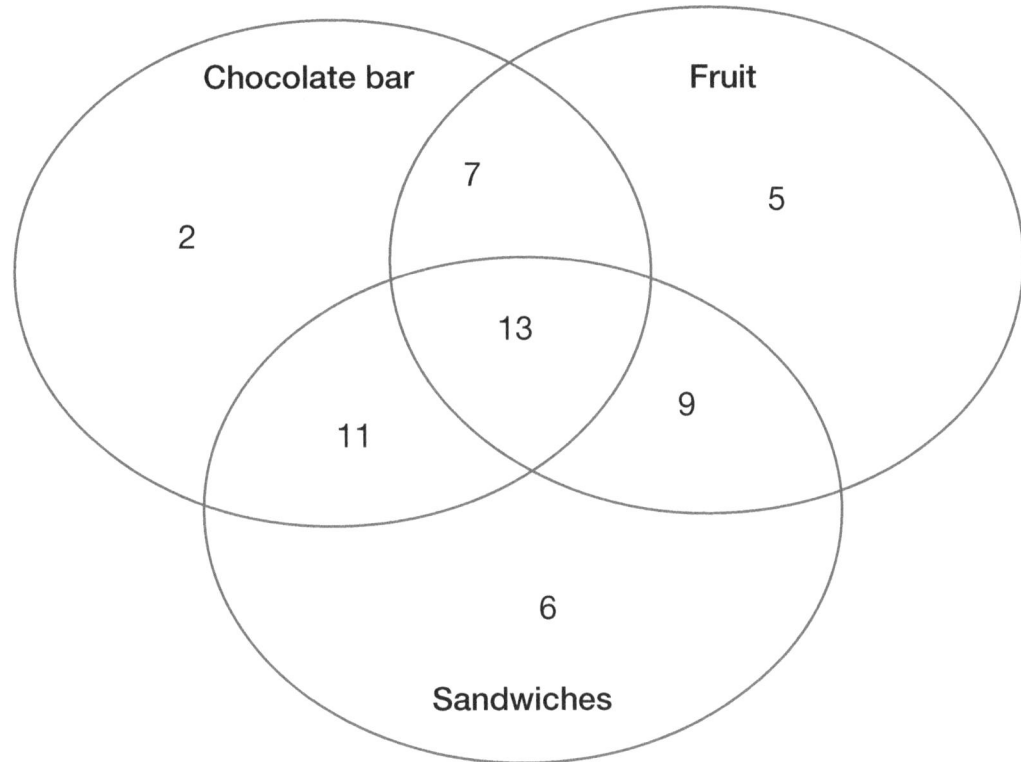

a) How many people had sandwiches and fruit in their lunchboxes?

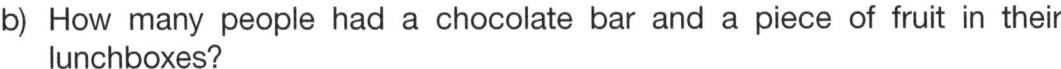

b) How many people had a chocolate bar and a piece of fruit in their lunchboxes?

c) How many people took part in this study?

QUESTION 8

Below is a comparative stem and leaf diagram showing the test scores for both men and women. The test was scored out of 100.

MALE		FEMALE
4	0	6 7 9
5 5 3 2	1	2 3 3 4
9 9 5 3 1	2	0 1
7 7 7 6 1	3	2 3 8 8 9
6 3 3 1 0 0	4	1 1 5 9
2 2	5	2 6 6 6 6
7 1 1	6	0 1
5	7	5 6
4 3 0 0	8	2 8 9
8 1 0	9	1 2 2 6

a) How many people took part in this survey?

b) Calculate the mean test score for women.

c) What is the difference between the range test scores for both men and women?

PICTOGRAMS AND OTHER USEFUL DIAGRAMS

Answers

Q1.

a) 23

(Highest value subtract the lowest value = 26 − 3 = 23)

b) 9, 12, 18

(All three of these values occur the most.)

c) 14

(Add up all of the numbers, and then divide it by how many numbers there are.)

- 420 ÷ 30 = 14

d) 12

(12 is the middle number.)

Q2.

a) 9

There are four whole shooting stars (equivalent to 8), and one half a star (equivalent to 1). So, 8 + 1 = 9

b) 2

The average number of shooting stars seen between January and March is 2. If 6 shooting stars were seen across the three months that means 6 ÷ 3 = 2

c) 28

Andy saw 28 shooting stars in total.

d) 21

You need to add up all of the shooting stars between the months April – June and July – September.

Q3.

	Even	Odd
Prime Numbers	2	7, 11, 17, 31
Not Prime	26, 42, 90	9, 49, 55

Q4.

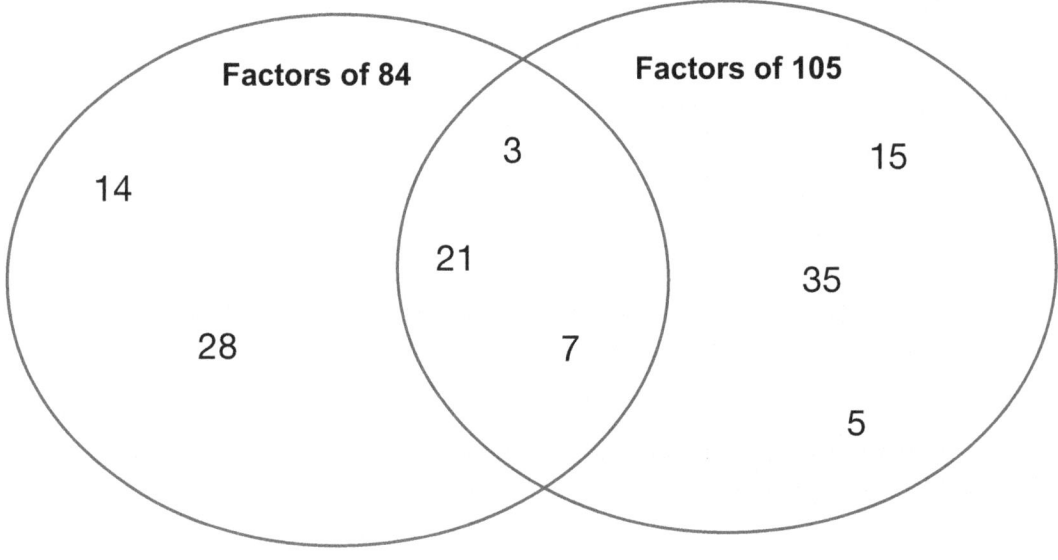

PICTOGRAMS AND OTHER USEFUL DIAGRAMS

Q5.

a)

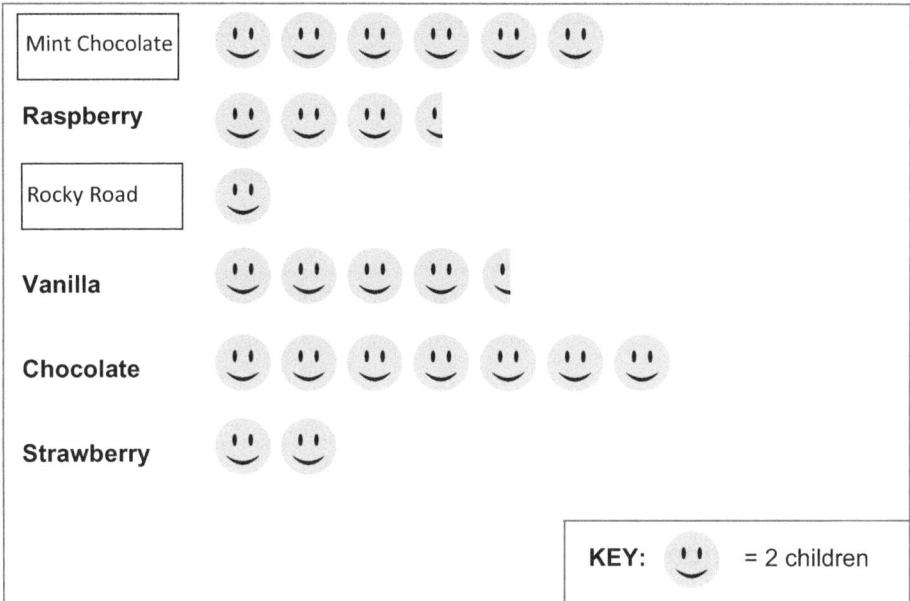

b) 48

(All you need to do is add up all of the frequencies in the table.)

c) Mint Chocolate

The most popular flavour was chocolate. The second most popular was mint chocolate.

Q6.

	Factors of 36	Factors of 40
Numbers between 1 - 10	6, 9	8, 5, 10
Numbers between 11 - 20	12, 18	20

Q7.

a) 9

(You need to focus on the number in the overlap between sandwiches and fruit.)

b) 7

(You need to focus on the number in the overlap between chocolate bars and fruit.)

c) 53

(Add up all of the numbers.)

Q8.

a) 68

(Add up how many numbers that are in the male AND female sections of the stem and leaf diagram.)

b) 48.5

(Add up all of the numbers for the female section, and then divide it by how many numbers there are. Remember that the test scores need to be added based on the STEM and LEAF values.

- Total = 1,649
- 1,649 ÷ 34 (total number of females) = 48.5

c) 4

- Range for women = 96 − 6 = 90
- Range for men = 98 − 4 = 94
- So, the difference is 4.

HOW ARE YOU GETTING ON?

NEED A LITTLE EXTRA HELP WITH KEY STAGE THREE (KS3) MATHS?

How2Become have created these other FANTASTIC guides to help you and your child prepare for their Key Stage Three (KS3) Maths assessments.

FOR MORE INFORMATION ON OUR KEY STAGE 3 (KS3) MATHS GUIDES, PLEASE CHECK OUT THE FOLLOWING:

WWW.HOW2BECOME.COM

WANT TO TAKE A LOOK AT OUR KEY STAGE (KS3) ENGLISH GUIDES?

How2Become have created these other FANTASTIC guides to help you and your child prepare for their Key Stage Three (KS3) English assessments.

FOR MORE INFORMATION ON OUR KEY STAGE 3 (KS3) ENGLISH GUIDES, PLEASE CHECK OUT THE FOLLOWING:

WWW.HOW2BECOME.COM

Get Access To
FREE
Key Stage 3 Resources

www.MyEducationalTests.co.uk

Printed and bound by CPI Group (UK) Ltd, Croydon, CR0 4YY
29/07/2025
01926316-0004